Twenty-six tales of genius, struggle, perseverance and heroism

Movers
& Shakers

Deaf People Who Changed the World

Cathryn Carroll & Susan M. Mather

DAWNSIGNPRESS
San Diego, California

Manufactured in the United States of America
Published by DawnSignPress
Illustrations by: Paul Setzer, Cynthia Sparks Cesone, and Shawn Richardson

Library of Congress Cataloging-in-Publication Data

Carroll, Cathryn
    Movers & shakers : deaf people who changed the world : storybook /
Cathryn Carroll & Susan M. Mather.
        p.   cm.
    Includes bibliographical references.
    ISBN: 978-0-915035-64-9

    1. Deaf--Biography.   I. Mozzer-Mather, Susan.   II. Title.
HV2373.C37   1997
362.4'2'0922--dc21
[B]   97-1408
                                                                 CIP

10   9   8   7   6   5

ATTENTION: SCHOOLS & DISTRIBUTORS

Quantity discounts for schools and bookstores are available.
For information, please contact:

DAWNSIGNPRESS

6130 Nancy Ridge Drive
San Diego, CA 92121
858-768-0428 VP • 858-625-0600 V • 858-625-2336 FAX
www.dawnsign.com

Table of Contents

In Appreciation

We wish to express our appreciation to Carolyn Jones, Gallaudet librarian; Deborah Sonnenstrahl, Art Department; Eric Malzkuhn, teacher, actor, writer, and signmaster extraordinaire; Gallaudet professors Marius Titus, Seth O'Cloo, Gabriel Adepoju, Harry Markowicz, Yerker Andersson, and Mark Weinberg; lecturer Paddy Ladd; archivists Ulf Hedberg and Mike Olson; artists Chuck Baird, Betty Miller, Paul Johnson, and William Sparks; photographers Chun Louie and Joan Schlub; sportswriter Barry Strassler; and the wonderful professors and researchers at the Smithsonian Institution and the University of Maryland for helping us to select and flesh out the individuals whose lives we portrayed.

Thanks also to teachers Melvia Miller-Nomeland and Yetti Sinnreich, from Kendall Demonstration Elementary School; Jim Barrie from the Model Secondary School for the Deaf; and Bette Landish, Mary Louise Guinta, Robert Clover Johnson, and Lisa Jacobs from Gallaudet University, for their time and effort in reviewing our material. In addition, we'd like to thank Marilyn Galloway, Julia Robertson, Sue O'Brien, Jean Clark, Marteal Pitts, Janne Harrelson, Susan Flanigan, Mary Abrams, and Kathleen Nowlan for their personal support. We also thank the Mather family—husband Bob, daughter Roberta, son Sam, niece Connie, and Sue's mother Helen Mozzer—as well as family friend Mei Yeh—for their comments on our materials.

Lastly, we want to thank the skilled and dedicated team at DawnSignPress and our gifted artists, Paul Setzer, Cynthia Sparks Cesone, and Shawn Richardson, for making this book possible.

Foreword

T his is a fascinating book about very unique people . . . people whose lives were challenged either by accident or circumstance, and how they met their challenges, overcame them, and/or used them to their advantage. These stories should be an inspiration to all of us.

This is a book specifically about deaf, hard-of-hearing, and deaf-blind individuals all over the world. It is a collection of success stories about, with a few exceptions, people many of us have never known. This book will give the unfamiliar reader an important insight into what it is like to live in a world without sight and/or sound.

This collection of short biographical stories is timely because it appears at a period in our history when the world-at-large is just beginning to recognize and accept diversity and learn more about the deaf community, our sign language, our culture, our history and some of the many contributions we have made to the world in which we live.

The reader cannot read these stories without feeling a sense of awe and admiration for the human spirit. Here is a sampling of successful achievers that will, or should, challenge deaf and hearing persons alike. We all want to make a difference in the world. Here are some individuals who did just that.

Another interesting note about this book is that not only is it a book about deaf people . . . researched and written by a team of deaf and hearing authors, but it was also illustrated by deaf artists and published by deaf publishers!

This book should appeal to many, but especially to young deaf people who are beginning to think seriously about their future, and those individuals who are still struggling to accept their deafness and wonder what their future holds. For the young deaf, hard-of-hearing, or deaf-blind person, I believe these stories will not only be of interest, but convince them that no one can hold them back . . . except themselves.

While the achievements of these individuals who helped change the world will not surprise many of us deaf people, they will nevertheless inspire us, and their success will increase our pride in our fellow deaf citizens of the world. These stories prove something we have always known, and something best put into words by Gallaudet University President I. King Jordan: "Deaf people can do anything . . . except hear!"

Jack R. Gannon, Author
Deaf Heritage

Introduction

In this book, we chronicle tales from the lives of some extraordinary individuals who changed the society around them and the world we live in today. All of them happened to have been deaf.

Of course, all of us change the world just by being born and living in it. Our selections and portrayals of individuals for this book were guided by our desire to note "impact and accomplishment" throughout the ages.

In addition, we were sometimes guided simply by what we were able to unearth from the past. For a few individuals there was a plethora of information. For example, Thomas Edison, America's foremost inventor who prized his deafness, is mentioned in a myriad of books and has several museums dedicated to him. For other individuals little published material was available. In the case of missionary educator Andrew Foster, who founded more schools for deaf children than anyone else in history, we were able to interview people who lived and worked with him. But astute readers may wonder why we did not write more about the order of nuns created by Princess Alice and more about the childhood of Black Coyote. Like many of the people we selected, these nuns were portrayed by writers who were interested in other matters. Thus the princess and the Sioux warrior appear briefly in the historical record and disappear. Yet their stories are too wondrous, their impact too great, to permit us to ignore their lives.

We also feel a need to explain why we did not capitalize the word "deaf." We simply felt it would be unfair to apply a standard that exists today to people who lived in a distant time. Clearly some of our characters—William Hoy, for example, who scribbled out his coveted autographs, always adding the initials D.M. for "deaf mute"—might reach out from the grave to embrace the capitalization. Others such as Ludwig van Beethoven, who hated being drawn into a condition that conflicted with his love and talent, might resist it.

We hope that all readers—deaf and hearing—draw inspiration from these tales of genius, struggle, perseverance, and often heroism. We feel that the lives we have chosen exemplify the quote affirmed so successfully by Dr. I. King Jordan, President of Gallaudet University: "Deaf people can do anything . . . except hear!" As these stories illustrate, despite hearing prejudice and communication barriers, deaf people have been doing it for a long time. We hope that these stories are a tribute to all of them.

Cathryn Carroll & Susan M. Mather

Movers & Shakers

Shakers

Deaf People Who Changed the World

Alice of Battenberg
1885-1969

When war came to Greece, the grandmother
of Prince Charles stayed in Athens
to take care of the orphaned children.

Glimpse of a Deaf Princess

IN THE EARLY morning hours of February 25, 1885, Queen Victoria held the hand of Princess Victoria, her first and favorite granddaughter, as the Princess gave birth to a little girl. They named the new baby Princess Victoria Alice Elizabeth Julie Marie. Everyone called her "Princess Alice." She was Queen Victoria's first great-grandchild and she was born deaf.

It was not unusual to have a deaf child in the British royal families. In 1253, a deaf princess, Katherine Plantagenet, was born to England's King Henry VIII and his wife. In Scotland, King James's daughter, Jean, was deaf. In Spain, Prince Don Jaime of Bourbon and his sister Princess Maria Christina were deaf. Several English dukes and earls were also deaf.

Princess Alice's aunt Alexandra, who became the wife of King Edward VII, was deaf, too. Often Alexandra went to the deaf church in London, sometimes dragging her husband with her. A fluent fingerspeller, Alexandra enjoyed the company of other deaf people there. Queen Victoria knew fingerspelling, too. Alice surely knew signs and fingerspelling. But, like most of the deaf members of the royal family, she was also trained to communicate using speech and lipreading.

With blond hair and brown eyes, Alice grew to be a beautiful woman. Perhaps that was why Prince Andrew of Greece fell in love with her. She was 17 years old and studying German in Germany when they met. Prince Andrew was 20 years old and visiting his German cousins. Prince Andrew always preferred to speak Greek, but surely he tried to speak English and German with the young girl who would become his bride.

When Alice returned to England and Andrew to Greece, they wrote to each other every day. One special day Alice received five letters. Prince Andrew wanted to marry her. Following custom, the Prince asked Alice's father, Prince Louis of Battenberg, for permission. Prince Louis discussed the possibility with the rest of the royal family. "No throne in Europe is too good for her," King Edward VII is reported to have said, as he ruffled Alice's hair.

The Wedding

The family agreed to the marriage, and the royalty of Europe gathered in Germany for the happy occasion. Princess Alice had three weddings! She was married under civil law, married in a Protestant church, and married in a Greek Orthodox church.

For each wedding, Alice carefully learned what she was to say and when she was to say it. All went well during the first two ceremonies. Then it was time for the Greek Orthodox ceremony. Alice was not familiar with the Greek Orthodox religion, and the priest wore a heavy beard that covered his lips.

Alice had memorized her role carefully. It was a simple role for a princess. She had to answer two questions, saying two words. When the priest asked if she had

Baby Princess Alice sits on the lap of her mother, Princess Victoria, while her aunt Beatrice stands behind them and her great-grandmother, Queen Victoria, smiles.

promised to marry another man, she was supposed to say "No." When the priest asked if she wanted to become the wife of Prince Andrew, she was supposed to say "Yes."

Perhaps tired after two ceremonies and so much partying, Alice mixed up the words.

"Have you promised to marry another man?" asked the priest.

That's when Alice was to say "No."

"Yes!" she said in a voice that echoed loudly through the church. Prince Andrew's brother nudged her, but it was too late.

"Do you wish to marry Prince Andrew?" continued the priest, ignoring her mistake.

Now Alice was supposed to say "Yes."

"No!" she said clearly, to another nudge from the elbow of the prince at her side.

Despite these mistakes, the wedding and partying continued. Alice's deaf aunt Alexandra had become queen after Queen Victoria's death in 1901. Queen Alexandra sparkled throughout the ceremony in her gown of amethyst sequins. Tsar Nicholas and

Tsarina Alexandra of Russia, Alice's uncle and aunt, came with the Russian Imperial Choir. Dozens of grand dukes, kings, queens, princes, and princesses celebrated, too.

As Alice and Andrew pulled away in their wedding carriage, the Tsar threw a satin slipper at the couple and it hit the bride. Alice turned around and angrily scolded him while the Tsar backed away, shaking with laughter.

No one knew it, but the wedding was the last time the royalty of Europe would get together on such a grand scale for such a happy occasion. War was coming to Europe.

Someone snapped a photo of Alice, Andrew, and their favorite wedding guests. By the end of World War I, half the guests in the photo were dead.

War!

Alice traveled with her new husband to Greece. There they lived in the Old Royal Palace in Athens, and Alice had a deaf lady-in-waiting. She began to learn the Greek language and Greek embroidery.

In 1905, she had her first child, Princess Margarita. Then Alice bore three more children, all girls—Princesses Theodora, Cecile, and Sophie. Sophie was born in 1914, the same year that World War I broke out.

Ruling Greece was never an easy job. In 1913, King George, Prince Andrew's father, was shot and killed. When they learned the news, Constantine, Andrew's brother and the new ruler of Greece, and his wife broke into tears. Princess Alice was the first in the room to comfort them. She put her arms around them, gave them a hug, and promised that everything would be okay.

But Princess Alice could not keep her promise. By now, the world was at war. When King Constantine refused to support the Allies in the war, they forced him to abdicate and let his son, Alexander, become king. In 1917, Alexander led Greece into World War I. Alice tried to keep her family safe as fighting broke out on the streets of Athens. She hid her daughters in the cellar of the Old Palace while fighting raged around them.

In 1918, World War I ended, but peace did not come to Greece. King Constantine returned and led Greece in an attack on Turkey. Alice tried to take care of her family while Andrew helped to command the Greek army. In 1921, she gave birth to her fifth child. It was her first boy. They named him Prince Philip.

Soon afterward, Alice's father died, and she returned to London for his funeral. She took tiny Prince Philip with her. But while she was in London, disaster struck. The Turks easily defeated the Greek army.

Alice hurried back to Greece to find soldiers guarding her home. She learned that the Greek military leaders blamed the royal government for their defeat. The soldiers arrested all royal leaders, including Prince Andrew, put them in jail, and accused them of treason.

Alice was desperate to see her husband. But the soldiers would not allow Prince Andrew to see anyone. They kept him alone in a cell and fed him only water and bread. The bread was so hard that Andrew broke a tooth when he tried to eat it.

Terrified, Princess Alice wrote to everyone, including the kings of England and Spain. "Help my husband," she begged.

Slowly the kings responded, asking the Greek soldiers to spare the life of the imprisoned prince. Alice and the kings were successful. Everyone who had worked under King Alexander was shot and killed—except

Princess Alice and her son, Philip

Prince Andrew. The soldiers spared his life and set him free. Andrew hurried to Alice and his children. The family boarded a British ship and escaped from the troubled country.

A Life Apart

Forced out of Greece, Alice, Andrew, and their children moved to France. They were very poor. Their relatives gave them money and let them live on a floor of a house in Paris. Alice did embroidery and worked in a shop for Greek refugees.

The royal children were growing. Sophie married Prince Christopher of Hesse when she was 16 years old. Cecile married soon after. Then Margarita and Theodora found husbands. For a short time, young Prince Philip bicycled to a nearby school. Then he was sent to boarding school in Germany.

As her children grew, Alice began to feel that she and her husband had grown apart. Even though her family was very important to her, she didn't want to live with him anymore. Prince Andrew loved parties, laughter, and good times. Alice was more serious. She was studying religion.

The prince and princess decided to live separately. Prince Andrew went to a fun-filled resort town in southern France. Princess Alice went to an island near Greece where she founded a nursing order of nuns.

Archive Photos

An aging Princess Alice, dressed in her nun's clothing, watches the face of her son Prince Philip carefully as the two converse.

When World War II broke out, Alice returned to Athens. The Germans attacked Greece and took over the country. Her family begged her to leave. At first, Princess Alice refused. She stayed in Athens during the German occupation, taking care of orphaned children.

When Alice returned to London, she maintained a religious life, almost always wearing her nun's clothing.

In 1947, Princess Alice's son, Philip, married Princess Elizabeth, the woman who would become the Queen of England.

Princess Alice died in 1969, at 84, in Buckingham Palace.

Ludwig van Beethoven
1770-1827

*Unable to hear it, this deaf man wrote some of
the greatest music the world has ever known.*

When a Mind Heard

ABOUT HALFWAY THROUGH the music, the conductor suddenly stopped the orchestra. He could see that the musicians were confused, as if something were wrong. The conductor pulled out one of the books that he used to communicate with people.

"What's wrong?" he asked, and he handed the little book to a friend so the man could write an answer. Perhaps his friend hesitated before he wrote. Finally he scrawled his words across the empty page, "It's no good anymore," he said.

The conductor, Ludwig van Beethoven, understood. Not even Beethoven, already known to be one of the greatest musical geniuses that ever lived, could conduct music that he could not hear, even when he had written it himself.

Mystery of Music

Who can explain the magical beauty of music? "A painting for the ears," one hearing person called it, "a language of emotions and beauty." Whether or not they hear, most people know little about music. Some people can sing a few songs, while others can play songs on musical instruments. Very few people can actually write music.

From the time he was a little boy, Beethoven was one of the most talented writers of music that ever lived. He began writing music when he was 12 years old. He became famous almost immediately, writing music and playing piano for royalty in Bonn, Germany, where he was born. In 1792, he moved to Vienna, Austria. In Vienna, he wrote music, gave concerts, and taught princes and princesses how to play the piano.

In the 1800s, concerts were all-day affairs. Beethoven would begin rehearsing with the orchestra in the morning and continue until the moment the concert began in the evening. Sometimes he would not even have time to write down the piano music and he would play his part from memory.

Beethoven was one of the first composers in the world to make a lot of money. Before Beethoven, composers were considered servants. They dressed like servants and they were expected to act like servants. Like cooks and butlers, they belonged to the royal households where they worked.

Beethoven was different.

"I ask and they give it to me," he wrote. He was the world's first musical celebrity. Princes, princesses, counts, lords, dukes, duchesses, and the royalty of Europe let him do what he wanted to do. They simply knew that he was a genius.

Fading Hearing

Beethoven started to lose his hearing when he was a young man. At first, he tried to hide it. He sat near the orchestra to try to hear the music better. But even next to the loudest instruments, he could only hear part of the sound. He admitted to a friend that he never heard high notes no matter where he sat.

Beethoven tried many cures and devices, such as ear trumpets, to improve his hearing. They didn't work; he threw them away. He spent one summer in the village of Heiligenstadt, outside of Vienna. He hoped the fresh country air would cure him. Nothing helped.

In his frustration and despair, he thought about killing himself. "I am an exile," he wrote. "What will become of me? Heaven alone knows."

Composing music, even when he could not hear it himself.

The beauty faded from his piano playing. Beethoven stopped playing in public, and eventually he stopped conducting. But he continued to write music, and many people feel that some of his best music was written after he became deaf.

From 1800 to 1815, Beethoven wrote six symphonies, two piano concertos, 14 piano sonatas, and a violin concerto. Later he wrote oratorios, an opera, and string quartets. His Third Symphony, the *Eroica*, was the longest piece of music ever written.

His famous Fifth Symphony begins with the notes da-da-da-dah! If the sound were transposed to the dots and dashes of Morse code, it would be dot-dot-dot-dash, the letter *V*. During World War II, the U.S. and its Allies used the notes as a secret "V-for-Victory" symbol.

Great Genius

Even as he struggled to hear, Beethoven began to accept his deafness. In 1814, Aloys Weissenbach, a deaf surgeon and poet, wrote the words to "The Glorious Moment," one of Beethoven's songs.

By 1818, Beethoven carried books of blank paper. He used the books to converse with people. Beethoven would talk with his voice and the other person would respond by writing in the books. He called the books his "conversation books."

Some people did not understand Beethoven's music, especially the music he wrote as he grew older. Once someone asked Beethoven if the notes he instructed the orchestra to make were really music at all. "Not for you," responded Beethoven, who realized his music was too complex for many people. "It is music for a later time."

Although they didn't understand him, people still adored the composer and his strange, exciting music. In 1824, Beethoven wrote and helped to conduct his famous Ninth Symphony. As the last notes faded, Beethoven remained facing the musicians.

At last a singer stepped forward, took his sleeve, and turned him gently to face the audience. Perhaps Beethoven was surprised to see the uproar. People were standing, clapping, and shouting. Over and over, their lips formed one word: "Bravo!"

The Ninth Symphony would prove to be the last symphony that Beethoven wrote. Today it is recognized as one of the greatest pieces of music in the world. After Beethoven's death, other renown composers—Mahler, Dvorak, Bruckner, Sibelius—found themselves so awed by it, that it is said they refused to write more than nine symphonies in deference to Beethoven.

Cynthia Sparks Cesone

Communicating with a friend in a conversation book.

10

Cynthia Sparks Cesone

To get Beethoven's attention, people often tapped him on the shoulder.

Music experts say that Beethoven's music reflects the great intuitions of humanity: that people everywhere are part of one family; that it is important to love one's neighbor; that nature is wondrous and beautiful; and that there is an all-loving God who doesn't belong to any one religion or group of people.

Beethoven died in Vienna in 1827 during a terrible storm. As the lightning flashed outside his window, he looked at those who kept watch at his sick bed and told them, "I will hear in heaven."

Shawn Richardson

Black Coyote
1860-1893

This Indian warrior may have begun
the Battle of Wounded Knee.

The Price of Refusal

IT WAS THE winter of 1893 when Black Coyote, the deaf Minnenconjou warrior, awoke to find his camp surrounded by United States soldiers. Black Coyote was 33 years old. He traveled with his wife, Brown Hair, and his baby daughter, Brings White. They were part of a small band of Indians travelling across the Dakota Territory to the camp of Chief Red Cloud. Seeing the U.S soldiers the night before, the Indians—mostly families of Sioux—raised a white flag and surrendered.

The soldiers wanted the Indian warriors to give up their weapons. "Throw down your rifles," the general ordered. While their women and children watched, the men tossed their rifles into a pile in the center of the camp. The Indians were upset. "We are not children to be talked to like this!" a warrior cried. Big Foot, their leader, counselled patience. "Take courage," he said.

Good Thunder, the Medicine Man, began a ghost dance. The Indians believed that the ghost dance would protect them, make the white people disappear, and the buffalo return. The white people feared the ghost dance and they had outlawed it. Watching Good Thunder, the soldiers were furious. They approached Black Coyote and demanded his gun.

It was a new Winchester rifle and Black Coyote was proud of it. He held it over his head for a moment in protest. The soldiers grabbed him and yanked the gun from his hands.

No one is sure who fired the first shot. Perhaps it was another Indian. Perhaps it was a soldier.

Perhaps it was Black Coyote.

At the sharp crack, all of the soldiers opened fired. Some of the Indians tried to reach for their guns, and many tried to protect their wives and children. But it was too late. The Indians began running and the soldiers chased them. "They shot us like buffalo," one Indian said later. In a few minutes, 350 Indian people—men, women, and children—lay dead on the frozen ground. Black Coyote's body was among them. It is not known what

"Put down your gun!" the soldier demanded.

happened to his wife and daughter. Brown Hair is listed as possibly killed. Scattered among the bodies were 25 dead soldiers, most of them shot by other soldiers.

The massacre became known as the Battle of Wounded Knee, the last major conflict in the American-Indian wars. After that, the land around Wounded Knee Creek became part of the United States. Today it is part of the Pine Ridge Indian Reservation in South Dakota.

James "Deaf" Burke
1808-1845

Before rules tamed boxing, this deaf orphan
fought barehanded to become the world champion.

Slugging to the Top

IT WAS 1833 and the fight for the championship of the world was underway. The men in the ring pummeled each other with their bare fists. Simon Byrne, an Irishman, and James Burke, an Englishman, had been fighting for three hours and 16 minutes, the longest championship fight in the history of boxing. Both of them were covered with sweat and blood.

Finally Burke landed a strong punch and Byrne collapsed. The crowd roared its approval. Burke, the man everyone called "Deaf Un" because he had been deaf for as long as he could remember, was the new prize-fighting champion of the world.

Burke's celebration was short-lived; however, because Byrne never got up. He was carried out of the ring unconscious. For three days, he lay in a coma. Then he died.

Perhaps all of Burke's championship glory suddenly felt hollow. He was arrested and his fight was investigated. In those days, there were few rules. Men fought without helmets or gloves, often beating each other to bloody unconsciousness. Doctors and lawyers agreed that Burke had fought a fair fight; he had done nothing wrong.

Burke was set free, but some people say that he still felt people looked at him as if he were a murderer. Within a few days he fled his homeland, sailing to America.

No Parents, No Home

Burke was no stranger to struggle and tough times. He had been born very poor. His mother and father had died when he was still a little boy. He never went to school and never learned to read or write. An orphan, he roamed the London waterfront, doing any work he could find, communicating through gestures and signs, and trying to stay out of trouble.

When he was 16 years old, Burke wandered into a bar called the "Spotted Dog." The owner, Joe Parrish, was a veteran fighter. Parrish liked young Burke and immediately saw that he might become a good fighter. Parrish became his trainer, teaching Burke the skills and tricks of prize-fighting.

When Burke was 18, Parrish let him have his first real fight. Now fights are limited to 12 rounds, but in those days, fights had no time limit. Burke and his opponent fought each other until the sun set. When referees finally stopped the fight, the two men had fought 50 rounds, and young Burke had shown himself as skilled and courageous as any fighter in Britain.

Burke was not a large man. Standing only five-feet-eight-and-a-half inches, he was nevertheless unintimidated by bigger men. He kept on fighting, winning three out of four fights during his first year. His fans loved him.

Burke showed courage during his fighting matches and in other ways. One day he saw flames shooting from a nearby house. As the blaze roared, he ran into the house to see if he could help anyone inside. He returned with a small child. Always tenacious, Burke returned again and again to the burning house. He brought out another child, then a woman, and then two more children. Unfortunately one of the children died in his arms. But the others survived and Burke became a hero.

Carrying a child out of the burning building.

His fights continued and he began to face fighters who were well known. The fights were often brutal. In 1828, he fought 106 rounds against William Fitzmaurice. Later he lost to Bill Cousens after fighting 111 rounds with him. It was a rare defeat for Burke. In the next 10 years, he won every one of his fights, defeating all who challenged him in the ring.

When Jem Ward, the heavyweight champion, retired in 1833, Burke claimed his title. Then came the Byrne challenge, Burke's reaffirmation as the champion of the world, the unexpected death, and his flight to America.

In America

Some say that Burke was the first man to bring prize-fighting to the United States. As the world champion, Burke arrived in New Orleans already famous.

Samuel O'Rourke, an Irishman who said that he was a friend of the dead Byrne, challenged Burke to a fight immediately. O'Rourke bragged that he was a professional fighter, but when the two men climbed into the ring together, it was apparent that he had very little experience. Against Burke, O'Rourke was helpless. The skilled and well-seasoned Burke punched him at will.

Watching O'Rourke lose badly, many of his friends in the crowd became angry. Some of them pulled out knives. The ropes surrounding the ring were cut. Angrily, the crowd

Training with his coach and communicating in gestures.

surrounded the men. Burke grabbed a knife and fought his way to his horse. He galloped away from the furious mob and never returned to collect his prize money.

Burke made his way to New York City, where a man named Tom O'Connell challenged him. Burke accepted the challenge, fought O'Connell, and demolished him in minutes.

Soon after his O'Connell fight, Burke returned to England. There William "Bendigo" Thompson challenged him. Burke, who was no longer in good physical condition, was defeated by Thompson. He had been world champion for six years.

In 1845, he died of tuberculosis at 36 years old. In 1966, he was inducted into the Boxing Hall of Fame.

Laurent Clerc
1785-1869

He brought education to America's deaf children—
and a rich and expressive language of signs.

In This Sign

IN 1816, LAURENT Clerc, a young teacher in Paris, France, approached the American stranger who was visiting his school. The stranger was Thomas Hopkins Gallaudet, a minister who had come to France to study deaf education. Gallaudet worked at Clerc's school for several months, watching teachers work with students and trying to learn the best way to educate deaf children. He was finishing his work in Clerc's classroom.

Using gestures, signs, and writing, Clerc told Gallaudet his daring idea: Clerc wanted to come to America; he wanted to help set up an American school for deaf children.

Gallaudet was pleased. He had seen that Clerc knew as much as anyone in the world about teaching deaf students. Clerc taught the highest class in the Paris school. Further, he was deaf himself and a graduate of the school. Sophisticated and articulate, Clerc was a living example of the success of deaf education.

Gallaudet quickly agreed with Clerc's plan—and their agreement changed the history of deaf education forever.

Boy from La Balme

Laurent Clerc was born in La Balme, a village in France. He told people that he became deaf when he fell out of a chair near the fire in the kitchen of his home. The fall and the fire left a scar on his cheek and made him deaf, he said. He was two years old. As a little boy, Clerc played alone most of the time. He wandered in the fields and explored the caves above the river bank. Clerc and his brothers and sisters made up signs to communicate with each other and often used them at home, but communication with his parents and the other village children was impossible.

When he was 12 years old, his family learned about a school for deaf students in Paris. Unable to communicate with his parents, Clerc knew nothing about the school. He did not know why his suitcase was packed. He did not know why he had to dress in traveling clothes when no one else in his family seemed ready to travel. He was even more puzzled when his uncle showed up at his house and his mother cried as he climbed into the carriage and rode away.

The house in La Balme, France, where Clerc may have been born and lived until he went to the School for the Deaf in Paris.

The School

They traveled for several days. Perhaps Clerc was more excited than scared. But when his uncle left him at the new school in the big city, he was terrified. Alone in the office of the school's director, Clerc cried. "Why would they do this to me?" he wondered. "Why would they leave me alone? Why am I so far from my family and home?"

Jean Massieu, temporarily in charge of the school, comforted the young boy. Massieu had taught at the school for a long time and greeted many new students. He understood why Clerc was upset and he led him gently to see his new room and meet the other students. Massieu, the first deaf man Clerc had ever met, used gestures to talk with him. He also used the language of signs—a language Clerc had never seen before.

When Clerc met the students, they noticed right away that he had a scar on his face from the fall many years before. They stroked their own cheeks at the site of the scar to represent Clerc's name. A stroke with two fingers along the cheek became Clerc's name sign.

Clerc's homesickness passed quickly. He learned signs and got used to the school. He earned good grades, too, right from the start. He only had one problem: speech class. At first, Clerc must have been honored to be picked for speech class. Only the smartest boys in the school could participate in it. Clerc went during his lunch break, giving up his free time to learn how to make the sounds of the French language.

When the children saw Clerc, they touched their faces to show his scar—and Clerc had a name sign.

In class, Clerc sometimes mixed up the pronunciation of two letters— *d* and *t*. Both letters look the same on the lips, but *d* requires voice. *T* only requires pushing air through the lips.

In those days, teachers were very strict and punishments were severe. One day, when Clerc mixed up the sounds in class, the speech teacher smacked him in the face. Clerc's mouth slammed shut at the force of the blow, and he bit his tongue. In pain and anger, he refused to go back to class. He vowed he would never use his voice again, and he never did.

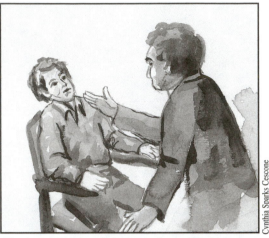

Clerc's mouth slammed shut at the force of the blow.

Despite his fury with speech class, Clerc came to love his school, the first national school for deaf students in the world. Clerc told people that it was his real home and that the students and teachers were his real family. When he graduated, he was happy to be offered a job as a teacher. When Gallaudet arrived at the school, Clerc had been teaching for 10 years.

The Decision

Perhaps Clerc thought that everyone would be happy with his decision to go to America. He was wrong. The Abbé Sicard, director of the school and Clerc's boss, tried to stop him. America was a terrible country, the Abbé Sicard said. Why, it practically belonged to the Indians! Almost equally horrible, it belonged to the Protestants. The Abbé Sicard and all the priests at the school were Catholic. In America, Clerc would lose his French culture and his Catholic religion, the Abbé worried. He wrote a note to Clerc's mother and begged her to convince her son to stay home.

Clerc persevered. Finally the teachers, students, and even the Abbé Sicard accepted his decision to go to America. Once they accepted it, they felt proud of him. "You will be the Apostle to the Deaf in the New World," Abbé Sicard told Clerc.

Sailing to America

In 1816, Clerc and Gallaudet boarded a boat and headed for America. The trip was extremely slow. The ship drifted in the ocean for hours, bouncing up and down on the ocean waves, without moving toward America. It took Clerc and Gallaudet 52 days to cross the Atlantic.

Clerc and Gallaudet didn't waste their time. They used their windless days to learn each other's language. Clerc taught Gallaudet sign language, while Gallaudet taught Clerc English. Clerc had studied English before. Now his study intensified. Everyday, he wrote in his diary, recording his journey in his new language. Gallaudet would read the diary every day and show Clerc his mistakes. Gallaudet thought that Clerc's English improved quickly.

When Clerc finally arrived in America, some people think that he was disappointed. Hartford, Connecticut must have seemed very small compared to Paris. Some people believe that Clerc was homesick, too. They say that Clerc would have returned to France immediately—if not for Alice Cogswell.

Meeting Alice

Alice Cogswell, the deaf daughter of the town doctor, was the reason that Gallaudet had gone to France in the first place. When Alice's father learned that there were no schools to teach deaf children in America, he and a group of Hartford businessmen paid for Gallaudet to go to England and France to learn about deaf education there.

Alice was 12 years old when Clerc arrived in Hartford. She had learned about Laurent Clerc from Gallaudet's letters and she was thrilled to finally see him in person.

While the other Americans greeted Clerc with a handshake, Alice welcomed him with a hug.

When Clerc and Gallaudet opened the school that would become the American School for the Deaf (ASD), Alice was one of their first students. Thirty-one students entered in the first year. One of the prettiest was a young girl named Eliza Boardman. When she graduated, Clerc asked her to marry him.

Gallaudet was upset that Clerc wanted to marry one of his students. Deaf people should not marry each other, Gallaudet said, because they might have deaf children. Clerc ignored his advice. Soon afterward Gallaudet copied Clerc. He married Sophia Fowler, another pretty ASD graduate!

Clerc taught at ASD for 41 years. He returned to France several times, visiting Jean Massieu and his other friends and their schools for deaf students. Massieu was surprised at how Clerc's signs had changed in America.

He laughed at Clerc. "Now you sign like an Indian," Massieu told him.

While Clerc traveled and taught, new schools for deaf students were established across the United States. Between 1817 and 1857, schools were founded in Kentucky, Pennsylvania, Tennessee, New York, Wisconsin, Michigan, Iowa, Virginia, Missouri, Georgia, Mississippi, Ohio, North Carolina, Indiana, and Washington, D.C.

THE OLDEST SCHOOL FOR THE DEAF IN THE UNITED STATES

Founded 1817
Thomas H. Gallaudet, of Hartford, first Principal.
Laurent Clerc, of Paris, France, first Instructor.

THOMAS H. GALLAUDET   1817   1821   LAURENT CLERC

Copyright by C. E. Emery, 1916.

THE AMERICAN SCHOOL FOR THE DEAF. HARTFORD. CONN.

A commemorative postcard from the American School for the Deaf, probably printed in the early 1900s, shows the school's founders and first locations.

Many of Clerc's students became teachers in the new schools. Clerc himself travelled to Philadelphia to become principal and teacher of the first class at the school that would become the Pennsylvania School for the Deaf. He worked there for seven months before he returned to the American School to continue teaching.

In the classrooms of the American School, the sign language that Clerc brought from France mingled with the signs of his students. As Clerc's students went to teach in the new schools for the deaf, they took their new American Sign Language with them. Partly because of the respect for the graduates of ASD, students throughout the United States would learn this American sign language and teach it to their students. Even today 58% of American signs come from the signs brought from France—and most of them arrived on the hands of Laurent Clerc.

The school names have changed over time; the names used here are those in current use.

Cynthia Sparks Cesone

LeRoy Colombo
1905-1974

Shawn Richardson

Alexander Ferguson
1841-1889

The American Colombo swam first to strengthen his own weakened leg muscles. He ended up becoming a lifeguard and saving 907 lives; the British Ferguson saved 55 people.

Champion Rescuers

IT WAS 1928, when LeRoy Colombo, a deaf lifeguard, saw the boat explode in the Gulf of Mexico near the town of Galveston, Texas. Horrified, Colombo watched as a fire broke out, burning the oil that spread over the troubled waters. Then he dove into the water, swam under the flames and made his way to the two crewmen. He was able to save both of them, pulling them beneath the burning flames to safety.

Colombo already had a reputation as a formidable lifeguard on the Texas coast. At 12, he made his first rescue, pulling a struggling child from the water. As years passed, he spent almost all his time near the water and often rescued people who were drowning. He became known as the "Hero of Galveston," credited with rescuing 907 people, an achievement that made the *Guinness Book of World Records*. At his death, the Texas Senate stopped working. Everyone stood for a moment of silence in his honor.

LeRoy Colombo, rescuer of over 900 people and the hero of Galveston, Texas, doing what he did best.

Colombo had learned to swim after an attack of meningitis left him weak, deaf, and almost paralyzed when he was seven years old. Every day, his brothers took him to the beach near their Galveston home, where he would swim to rebuild the strength in his legs. LeRoy continued swimming when he entered the Texas School

Colombo braved rough water to make his rescues.

for the Deaf at age 10. He stayed at TSD until his father died. Then he went to work to support his mother and the rest of his family.

Colombo had a counterpart in Alexander Ferguson, a deaf man who lived in Britain. When Ferguson pulled a drowning swimmer from the water at 10 years old, it was only the beginning of his life-saving career. Ferguson rescued a total of 55 people from the rivers of England, Scotland, and Ireland, winning money and medals for his achievement.

The two saviors of the water never met each other, but the children and grandchildren of people they rescued are grateful for the heroism of these extraordinary deaf lifeguards.

Cynthia Sparks Cesone

Joachim Du Bellay
1522-1560

Sick and forsaken, he found comfort in French,
his country's native language, defended it to the world,
and helped bring it into the literature of France.

Hymn to Deafness

"YOU COMPLAIN, RONSARD, of being deaf," wrote Joachim Du Bellay, French poet and humanist, as death drew near in 1558. But Du Bellay was not criticizing Ronsard, France's best poet and his own dear friend. Instead Du Bellay was praising Ronsard, as he always did.

Du Bellay and Ronsard were two of the best-known writers in France. While everyone agreed that Ronsard, the "Prince of Poets," was the foremost French writer, most people placed Du Bellay just after him. "Gentle Du Bellay," commented one of their friends, "and serious Ronsard."

Du Bellay and Ronsard both came from noble families. Both men were humanists. They loved to read ancient books in Latin and Greek. And they loved French, their own native language. Both men were deaf, too, having lost their hearing when they were young.

While they had much in common, the men were different from each other, too. Ronsard preferred to communicate with people through speech and lipreading. Du Bellay preferred to communicate through writing. While Ronsard preferred to ignore his deafness, Du Bellay wrote a 12-page poem about it. In his famous poem, *Hymn to Deafness*, Du Bellay wrote that being deaf had helped him become a poet. It helped Ronsard become a poet, too, Du Bellay wrote. For a poet, deafness might be a blessing, Du Bellay thought, even if it were a blessing in disguise.

While Ronsard was healthy, Du Bellay was often sick. When he was in his thirties, he became so sick that he went to bed and stayed there for two years.

Lonely Orphan

Perhaps Du Bellay was one of those people who is always a little bit sad. Both of his parents died when he was 10 years old. He went to live with his older brother, René. René was supposed to make sure that Du Bellay received an education, but Du Bellay said that he learned nothing while he lived with him. He often felt lonely. To make himself feel better, he took long walks. He enjoyed the beauty of the French countryside, and he began to write poetry.

Perhaps the best Latin poet in France, Du Bellay still preferred to write in French.

Cynthia Sparks Cesone

In 1543 one of Du Bellay's cousins died, and young Du Bellay went to the funeral. The cousin was very well known and many of France's best writers were at the funeral. Did Du Bellay meet them? Was he inspired? Ronsard, the deaf writer who would become his friend, was at the funeral. Did Du Bellay meet Ronsard there? No one really knows.

It is known that when he was old enough, Du Bellay went to the nearby city of Poitiers where there was a university. Perhaps he planned to study law. Perhaps he planned to study poetry. Again no one really knows. Du Bellay did not stay at the university for a long time.

Somehow Du Bellay had become friends with Ronsard, and perhaps it was Ronsard who told him about the new school in Paris. Ronsard was already going to the school—Collège de Coqueret. At the Collège de Coqueret, students learned Greek, read Latin, and wrote their own poetry in French.

Du Bellay joined Ronsard in Paris. There, for the first time, he met people whose interests were the same as his—students who loved the literature of Greece and Rome—and the language of France.

Guiding Lights

Du Bellay, Ronsard, and the other students at the school formed a group, almost like a club. They called themselves "La Pléiade." The Pleiades (in French "La Pléiade") is a cluster of stars that shine in the night sky, named after goddesses of ancient Greece. Like the night's shining Pleiades, the college students felt that they were the lights that all of France would follow.

In 1549, a Paris lawyer wrote a pamphlet called *Art Poetique Francoys*. The pamphlet called on French poets to follow in the tradition of Latin poetry. Du Bellay, Ronsard, and their friends in La Pléiade disagreed. They believed that good poems could be written in the French language, too. Someone must challenge the lawyer's ideas, the students decided.

They picked Du Bellay.

Du Bellay responded by writing a long essay called "The Defense and Glory of the Language of French." In the essay, Du Bellay described and defended his language. French could be powerful, precise, and beautiful, he maintained. It was every bit as good as Latin.

Du Bellay wrote quickly and emotionally. When his essay was published, French readers were thrilled. His essay became a statement for everyone in France. It represented French pride and patriotism.

Later in the year, Du Bellay wrote a book of poetry. He wrote about an imaginary woman whose name was Olive. Even though he was sick again and could not get out of bed, he made sure that his book was published.

In 1553, Du Bellay's cousin invited him to travel to Rome to work for him. Du Bellay was thrilled to be able to see Rome, the ancient city that was home to the Latin writers whom he loved so well. He and his cousin traveled through France to Italy, following the route that the French royal family took when it journeyed through France. As they crossed the mountains, Du Bellay fell sick with a high fever. The doctors, using the best medicine of the time, bled him. Du Bellay was very weak, but he continued his journey anyway.

When they arrived in Rome, Du Bellay was disappointed. Rome was very different from the city he had imagined. More than one thousand years had passed since the time of the famous Latin writers. He felt that the great capital was a city in decay, and it made him sad.

Du Bellay met Faustina.

Worse, Du Bellay did not enjoy working for his cousin. Du Bellay's job was to manage his cousin's house and staff and work as his cousin's secretary. Perhaps partly because deafness made communication difficult, he found his duties hard to carry out.

Unhappy and lonely, he missed France. He felt better when he met a woman named Faustina. But Faustina was married and her husband did not like her friendship with Du Bellay. He sent Faustina to a convent to live as a nun!

Poor Du Bellay. He was alone again. As usual, he helped himself feel better by writing poetry. He published many poems—most of them in Latin.

The man who loved his own French language so much became the best Latin poet in Europe.

He returned to Paris in 1558, writing poems and books in French and publishing translations of Latin poems.

His health continued to decline. In January, 1560, he returned from a friend's house and began to write poetry. He died as he wrote. He was 38 years old. His friends called a celebration in his honor. By this time, the language of French was loved and respected around the world, thanks partly to Du Bellay.

Thomas Alva Edison
1847-1931

He made light and recorded sound,
but America's foremost inventor refused
the technology that could make him hear.

Lighting Up the World

AS A LITTLE boy in the mid-1800s, Tom Edison was always in trouble. He gathered eggs from his family's chickens and sat on them to try to make them hatch. He was curious about fire, started one, and burned down his father's barn.

His parents punished him harshly. After he burned down the barn, his father marched him down to the town square and gave him a public whipping. His mother kept a switch just to spank her youngest son. But Tom's escapades continued.

When he was 10 years old, Tom made a young friend drink special chemicals. The chemicals produced gas inside his friend's body and he got so sick that he lay on the floor in great pain. Undoubtedly, young Tom Edison was upset. He had known that the chemicals would produce gas, but he thought that if his friend were filled with gas, he would be able to fly.

Further, Tom often had ear infections. At 7 years old, he had scarlet fever, too. As a result, his hearing declined. Sometimes he couldn't understand people unless he watched their lips; sometimes he couldn't understand them at all.

Some people thought that Tom Edison was stupid. His teachers called him "addled," which means stupid and a little bit crazy. Only his mother—despite her regular spankings—seemed to have faith in him. When she learned that the teachers had called her son addled, she took him out of school. She would teach her son at home.

For a while, Edison's mother did teach him at home. Mostly she just helped Tom to teach himself. She bought him a chemistry set and some books, and soon young Tom Edison was busy doing experiments. He didn't want his family to touch his chemicals, so he labeled all of them "POISON."

First Job

Edison was too restless and his family was too poor for him to stay at home. When he was 12 years old, Edison got a job working on trains. As the trains rolled from one town to another, he walked the aisles, selling candy, fruit, newspapers, and nuts. Sometimes the Edison family's only money came from young Tom. Perhaps that's partly why he never went back to school. Tom Edison attended school for only three months in his whole life.

Even at work, Edison could not stop experimenting. The conductor let him bring his chemicals on the train and experiment in the baggage car. Perhaps it was inevitable that an accident would happen. Sure enough, one day while Edison was experimenting, he accidentally started a fire. The conductor was furious. He hit Edison across his ears, threw him off the train, and fired him. After that, Edison could only sell his candy and newspapers in the train stations. When he grew up, Edison blamed the conductor's whack across the ears for his deafness.

One day as he worked in the train station, he noticed the station owner's

As a boy, Tom Edison loved to experiment and read.

son playing on the train tracks while a train rolled towards him. Edison pulled the boy to safety just in time. Grateful that he had saved his son's life, the boy's father agreed to teach Edison how to send telegrams.

Sending telegrams was an important skill in the 1800s. Soon Edison had his first real job. He was a telegrapher, sending messages in Morse code over telegraph lines. He worked in many towns, travelling throughout Canada and the United States. During his free time, he continued experimenting and inventing new things.

First Invention

At first, Edison's inventions did not make him rich or famous. In fact, one of his first inventions got him fired! During the night, telegraphers were supposed to report to their bosses every hour. Their bosses were in faraway cities, so the telegraphers tapped their reports over the telegraph lines. When the bosses received the reports, they knew that the men were at their desks and working.

Edison did not want to stay awake all night. So he invented an automatic reporting device. With an automatic reporting device, telegraphed messages were sent to his boss automatically. Each night Edison connected the device to the telegraph and went to sleep. All night long, the automatic reporting device would send messages to his boss every hour while Edison slept. He was sleeping soundly one night when the boss came to visit him. He was fired immediately.

In 1869, the 22-year-old Edison arrived in New York City with no money, no home, no family, and no job. He persuaded an employee of Gold Indicator, a company that sold and traded gold on Wall Street, to give him small jobs and let him sleep in a basement office.

A few days later, the stock ticker broke down. To everyone's astonishment, Edison, the deaf homeless man, was the only person who could fix it. Surprised at his skill, the boss offered Edison full-time employment. Edison accepted eagerly. Then he improved the boss's stock ticker so that it would not break down again.

Later, Edison and another man decided to start their own business. As they got ready to open it, Edison's former boss appeared and asked if he could buy the patents that Edison had earned for his inventions with the stock ticker. Edison was happy to sell the patents; he was very poor and needed money badly.

Cynthia Sparks Cesone

Alone and homeless, Edison arrived in New York City.

He was nervous though. Should he ask his old boss for $5000 or should he ask for $3000? He really wanted $5000 and he was sure that his boss could afford it, but he didn't want to make his boss angry and $3000 was still a lot of money. Unsure what to say, Edison asked his boss how much he would be willing to pay.

"Forty thousand dollars," his boss said.

Edison was shocked and elated. It was more money than he had ever seen in his whole life. He gripped the table tightly. "That would be fair," he said. With $40,000, he could be an inventor full time.

Perhaps feeling very rich, Edison asked a young woman to marry him. Her parents were nearby and he did not want them to hear him, so he tapped out his marriage proposal in Morse code on a coin. She tapped back her answer: Y-E-S.

As a constant worker, Edison left his bride on his wedding night to work on his invention.

The Phonograph

Why would a deaf man think about copying sounds that he could not hear? Few people even believed it was possible. How could you copy something you couldn't see? But Edison thought there must be a way. He drew his idea on paper and gave it to his assistant. "Make this," he told him.

His assistant followed Edison's instructions and made the strange machine. Then he brought it to his boss.

"What's it for?" the assistant asked Edison.

"This machine is going to talk," Edison told the astonished man. Then Edison shouted into the machine: "Mary had a little lamb." He wound it back and the machine repeated Edison's words.

Of course Edison heard nothing. He shook his head, ran his fingers through his hair, and wondered how he would make the machine a success.

Then he looked up. He saw that his assistants had turned white and were staring at the new machine as if it were a ghost. They had just heard the machine repeat Edison's words in a high fuzzy whine. "Mary had a little lamb," it had squeaked. Edison was the first person to make a copy of human sounds in history—and his assistants were the first people to hear it.

Light Bulb

The light bulb is probably Edison's most famous invention. Many people were trying to invent the light bulb, but Edison did it first. Then he invented generators to produce enough power to light whole cities at night.

In 1881, when he was 34 years old, Thomas Edison traveled to New York to light the first city streets. It wasn't until 1882 that his project was a success. "Genius is 10% inspiration and 90% perspiration," said Edison.

When he died at 84 years old, Edison had over 1,000 patents, more than any other inventor in U.S. history. In addition to the light bulb, power stations, and phonograph, Edison invented mimeographs, improved the telephone so it would work over long distances, and combined photos with sound to make the first simple movies.

But the genius of technology wanted no part of the technology that would alter his hearing. Edison refused an operation to make him hear. His deafness was an advantage, he said, it helped him concentrate. He preferred to be deaf, he said. He wanted it that way.

Cynthia Sparks Cesone

Juan Fernandez
Ximenes de Navarette
1526-1579

He painted for the king of Spain and
thousands still enjoy his work today.

Painting for the King

IN THE 1500s, Santayo came to see King Philip II of Spain. Santayo was King Philip's minister and advisor. He was also furious.

"Make him change it!" Santayo demanded. "It must be changed!"

King Philip knew what Santayo was talking about and perhaps he smiled at his minister's fury. Santayo, surprised at the king's attitude, lost his anger and began to plead with him. "Please make him change it!" he begged.

But King Philip shook his head. He had already seen the painting and he did not want the artist to change it at all. He thought it was perfect just the way it was. It would be beautiful on the wall of his new royal residence, the fabulous building that would become the Escorial.

The painting was typical of those of Juan Fernandez Ximenes de Navarette, the artist everyone called "El Mudo." It was huge and precise, yet warm, and filled with spirituality and human emotion. Called *The Execution of St. James*, it showed the death of a Christian martyr. Fernandez had painted it in a hurry because he knew that King Philip was anxious for the walls to be finished so that he could move into his new home.

In his painting, Fernandez had recreated an important moment from Christian history. St. James looked holy, and the executioner looked evil. Each figure in the painting stood exactly six feet tall, larger than the people who looked at it. Like many artists, Fernandez painted faces of people that he knew in his work. He thought that Santayo was arrogant and the two men had been feuding. Thus for the evil face of the executioner, he used as a model the face of the hated Santayo.

No wonder Santayo was upset! He realized that he had been painted as a murderer.

But King Philip adored his talented artist and he didn't mind Fernandez making fun of the pompous Santayo. Despite Santayo's pleas, King Philip never ordered Fernandez to change the picture.

Today many of Fernandez's paintings hang in the Escorial, the royal residence and burial place of Spanish kings and queens, near Madrid. One of the paintings is *The*

Execution of St. James, where the face of the executioner still bears a resemblance to the long-dead Santayo.

Talent for a Lifetime

Fernandez was born in 1526. He became deaf when he was three years old, probably from illness. He never spoke and he quickly earned the name "El Mudo," which means "the mute."

As a young boy, he was sent to live in a monastery. The monastery was the home of a "silent order" of monks. In silent orders, monks were limited in speaking. They often used sign language and fingerspelling. Fernandez learned to read, write, and do arithmetic in the monastery. He also began to learn the art of painting.

Santayo begged the king to make Fernandez change the painting, but King Philip just laughed.

He learned to paint so quickly and so well that his teacher suggested that he go to Italy and study painting. Fernandez stayed in Italy for about 20 years. In Italy, he learned to copy the great Italian painter, Titian. Later he became known as the Spanish Titian.

When he returned home to Spain, Fernandez made a painting of the baptism of Jesus and entered it in a competition with many other painters for a position on the royal payroll. The king loved his painting and Fernandez entered the royal service.

Artist with Humor

Fernandez had a good sense of humor. Even today, people talk about the humor that he incorporated into his work. For example, in one of Fernandez's religious pictures for the Escorial, he painted the Holy Family, crafting the figures of Joseph, Mary, and the baby Jesus with gentle spirituality. Then he moved his brush away from the family to show that even the most serious moments have a funny side. On one side of the painting, he drew a bird; and on the other side, he drew a cat and a dog fighting over a bone.

Fernandez was a perfectionist. Sometimes when he didn't like his work, he destroyed it. King Philip, who loved all Fernandez's paintings, usually tried to stop him. Once, the king was successful. Today people consider the painting King Philip saved one of Fernandez's best. It was *The Assumption*, a painting of Jesus' mother, Mary. For the face of the Mary, Fernandez painted the face of his own mother.

Fernandez used an interpreter with his friends.

Although King Philip usually let his favorite artist do whatever he wanted, Fernandez lost at least one argument with his monarch. A beautiful religious painting arrived at the royal palace, painted by the famous Titian, who was Fernandez's idol. But the painting was too big. Everyone was horrified when it did not fit on the wall.

The king decided to cut the painting to make it fit. Fernandez was horrified. Few people dared to argue with the king, but Fernandez did. He begged King Philip to leave the priceless painting in one piece. Using signs and gestures, he offered to copy the painting himself, promising that his copy would look just like the original—except it would be a bit smaller to fit into the proper space on the wall. But King Philip would not change his mind. He had the painting cut up, threw away some of its pieces, put the remainder of the pieces back together, and hung the reconstituted painting on his wall.

Fernandez used interpreters throughout his life to communicate with people who did not know sign language. No one knows who the interpreters were or how they were trained, but documents show that their presence and interpretations were accepted as legal. Fernandez's interpreters always took an oath before they worked for him, swearing to accurately represent the wishes of deaf and hearing people.

In 1571, Fernandez became seriously ill. For a short time, he returned to his home in Logrono, then he traveled back to Madrid. Finally he began his last paintings in Toledo. As he lay dying, Fernandez jotted down instructions for his will and tried to explain more through sign language. No interpreters were present and people were not sure that instructions conveyed only in sign language were legal. But they accepted what they believed were his wishes and carried them out when he died in 1579.

Andrew Foster
1925-1987

*His achievement was all the greater because the
first human rights he had to fight for were his own.*

Bringing Hope to Deaf Africans

IN 1947, a young man stood before Eric Malzkuhn, a vocational rehabilitation counselor in Flint, Michigan. His name was Andrew Foster. Foster was 17 years old, deaf, black, and one of the smartest people that Malzkuhn had ever seen in his office.

With test scores like Foster's, the teenager should be in school and getting ready for college, thought Malzkuhn. Instead he was working in a factory. A graduate of the Alabama School for the Colored Deaf, Foster had an 8th grade education. He had applied to the Michigan School for the Deaf (MSD), but MSD refused to accept him. Foster was not really a resident of Michigan, MSD said. His parents were in Alabama; therefore Foster was still a resident there.

Malzkuhn wondered if the reason had more to do with Foster's skin color. In Alabama, segregation by race was law. Black people could not eat, shop, or go to school with white people. But in 1947 Malzkuhn knew black people usually lived separate—and unequal—lives from white people, even in the northern state of Michigan.

Impressed with Foster's intelligence, Malzkuhn began to process papers for Foster to go to Gallaudet College, the college for deaf students in Washington, D.C. He was not surprised, however, when Gallaudet rejected him. Foster was not ready for college work, Gallaudet said. At Gallaudet, the policy was perhaps not quite "whites only" but certainly it was "whites mostly." Only one black student was there and Malzkuhn did not know of any African-American who had ever graduated.

Deaf himself, Malzkuhn knew that sometimes people have to prove they are better to be accepted as equal.

"You'll have to take some classes to prove to Gallaudet you can do it," he told Foster.

"What?! And give up my jobs?" demanded Foster. "Impossible!"

"Not give up your jobs," explained Malzkuhn. "You're going to do both—go to school and work your jobs."

That suited Foster just fine.

Working Man

Foster worked in restaurants, bakeries, laundries, machine shops, and aircraft and auto factories. He drove trucks and handled stock. At the same time, he took high-school correspondence courses from the American School in Chicago and night classes at the Detroit Institute of Commerce.

He thought about going into business. He thought about becoming a professional fighter. But Foster was deeply religious. Every Sunday, he went to a church where there were many deaf people. Often he stayed after church to discuss—even argue—with the minister. Foster wanted to know more about the Bible and he wanted to know more about God.

African Dream

One day at church, Foster met a missionary who had been to Jamaica, a poor island country in the Caribbean Sea. The missionary gave a speech about the difficult life of deaf Jamaicans.

As he watched the speech, Foster realized that deaf people in the U.S. were lucky compared to deaf people in the rest of the world. In America, deaf people—even deaf people who were black—could go to school. They could learn to read and write, and they could learn about God.

In 1951, Foster entered Gallaudet. Most students went to Gallaudet for five years. A year of preparation was followed by four years of college study. But Foster completed his education in three years, squeezing summer jobs around summer courses at the Hampton Institute in nearby Virginia. When asked his most memorable experiences at Gallaudet, Foster wrote, "just studied most of the time . . . "

At Gallaudet, Foster's goal came into focus. He read that there were only 12 schools for children with disabilities in Africa—12 schools in a land of 51 countries and half a billion people!

Foster studied long into the night, while his roommate slept.

Perhaps he was inspired by the missionary from Jamaica. Perhaps he was inspired by his own Christian beliefs. Foster decided to become a missionary and teach deaf children in Africa. But first, he had to prepare himself. In 1954, he graduated from Gallaudet College. He went to Eastern Michigan University and became the first black person there to earn a Master of Arts (MA) degree. Then he earned a third degree from Christian Missions College in Seattle, Washington.

Some people tried to discourage Foster from going to Africa. Missionaries, all of them hearing, told him there were very few deaf people there. They said that Africa was a land where everyone had trouble learning to read and write unless they were very rich and could pay for their education. Foster persisted. During his final year in Seattle, he organized the Christian Mission for Deaf Africans. In 1956, he left for Ghana, a small country on Africa's west coast.

In Africa

Foster's first school was set up in a small room borrowed from a church. Twelve students attended the first year and the school grew quickly. Soon Foster was on his way to setting up another school.

A deaf teenager, Gabriel Adepoju, later a professor at Gallaudet University, remembered Foster's arrival in Nigeria, a country that neighbors Ghana. "The newspaper said that a Dr. Andrew Foster had arrived in Nigeria and set up a school for deaf children," recalled Adepoju. The newspapers probably used the word "doctor" as a sign of respect.

Deafened from an attack of smallpox, Adepoju sat down and wrote Foster a letter. He told him that he had managed to finish high school, but now he had nowhere to go and nothing to do. Adepoju asked Foster for medicine to cure his deafness.

Foster wrote him back immediately. He said nothing about a cure. Rather, Foster invited Adepoju to his school. "Come see me," his letter said.

As soon as he could, Adepoju got on a bus and headed to the school. When the bus arrived, he was shocked by what he saw. In the schoolyard, deaf children were talking excitedly and they were using sign language. Adepoju had never seen sign language before. "They must be mentally retarded deaf children," he thought.

He made his way through the building to the school's headmaster and found a man seated at a large desk. Adepoju went up to him and used his best voice to explain that he was looking for Foster. The man stared at him. Finally the man touched his ears and shook his head.

"You're deaf!" exclaimed Adepoju, realizing the man could not hear him. "The same as me!"

The man nodded. The two men began to write notes back and forth. Foster was in Ghana, the headmaster explained, and he would be back the next day.

The next day Adepoju was there to greet Foster when the bus from Ghana pulled up near the school. Anxiously he watched as Andrew Foster got out of the bus. He was surprised at his size. At 6′1″, Foster towered over most people.

"He was big—like a football player," remembered Adepoju. He got up his courage and went to talk with him. Again he used his voice. Again, the same reaction: A touch to the ears, a shake of the head. Adepoju could not believe it.

"You are deaf!" he cried again.

Foster nodded and invited Adepoju to join him for lunch. Adepoju and Foster went to the lunch room to eat with the students. Before they ate, the students signed a prayer to give thanks for their food. Again Adepoju was stunned. "The deaf children knew to pray before they ate," marvelled Adepoju.

Standing in the school lunch room, Adepoju suddenly realized that he had been wrong. He had misjudged everything—the students, the school, and the great teacher from America. Perhaps more importantly, he had misjudged himself. There was nothing wrong with being deaf, he realized. There was no reason to be ashamed.

Foster showed him a small library in the school and Adepoju pulled out a sign language book. He remembers the first signs he learned. "GO, COME, DRINK," he said. "I learned those signs quick. I was hungry to communicate." When Foster asked Adepoju to become a teacher in his school, he accepted the offer.

In 1959, Foster went to a meeting of the World Federation of the Deaf. The first person he met there was a young German woman, Berta Zuther. Like Foster, Zuther wanted to be a missionary. Like Foster, she was deaf. Berta and Andrew Foster married in Nigeria in 1961. They had five children.

By 1968, Foster had set up five schools, two in Ghana and three in Nigeria. The Nigerian School in Ibadan soon had residential students and 300 students on the waiting list.

In the following two decades, Foster set up more schools in many African nations, including Benin, Cameroon, Central Africa Republic, Chad, Congo, Gabon, Ghana, Ivory Coast, Kenya, Niger, Nigeria, Senegal, Togo, Sierra Leone, Upper Volta, and Zaire. According to Adepoju and others, he set up over 30 schools, most of them affiliated with churches.

THE FOSTER FAMILY
BERTA   FAITH   ANDREW
JACKIE   FREDDY   TIM
Field: NIGERIA, WEST AFRICA

Bible logics:
How shall they call on Him in
whom they have not believed?
How shall they believe in Him of
whom they have not heard?
How shall they hear without
a preacher?
How shall they preach, except
they be sent?
— ROM. 10:13-17

Have you prayed for us today?

CHRISTIAN MISSION
FOR DEAF AFRICANS
P.O Box 1452
Detroit,
Mich, 48231
U. S. A.

Gallaudet University Archives

As a young father, Andrew Foster with his wife, Berta, and their children.

Andrew Foster works with students.

African Legacy

Before Andrew Foster arrived in Africa, many Africans believed that deafness was a curse from God. As a result, parents were ashamed of their deaf children and sometimes they hid them. Once in a while, they even abandoned them, leaving them alone to beg for food or to starve. When deaf adults came together, they often did not dare use their hands to talk with each other.

When he died in a plane crash in 1987, Foster left behind hundreds of deaf African children who were learning to read and write. He left behind educated deaf adult Africans, trained to teach their own people. And he left thousands of hearing people who realized that the deaf people they had mocked and shunned were every bit as smart as they were.

Although civil unrest and political change meant that some of Foster's schools would not survive, some continue today. In 1990, a group of high school students from the U.S. who visited Senegal were surprised to find that students at the Ephphatha School for the Deaf used American signs, and that Foster's picture was in the office of the school's director. "He is revered by all deaf Africans who knew or studied with him," noted their teacher, Marcia Freeman.

John Goodricke
1764-1786

He made discoveries about the stars and
awed the world's astronomers.

Exploring Star Light

IT WAS NOVEMBER 12, 1782, in York County, England. The minutes ticked slowly past midnight. Suddenly, 18-year-old John Goodricke gasped in amazement.

At first Goodricke thought he had made a mistake. Perhaps he was seeing things, or perhaps the air was bad. He looked through his telescope again.

Right in front of his eyes, a star had changed. The star was "Algol." Easily seen with the naked eye, Algol is the second brightest star in the constellation Perseus. Goodricke knew Algol well; scientists had studied it since ancient times.

The night before, when he had peered through his telescope, Goodricke saw that Algol was bright and shining. Its light measured at the second magnitude on the scale of brightness—just like the scientists said it should. But tonight, Algol was not bright at all. In fact, it was quite dim.

A stunned Goodricke applied his scientific instruments to measure Algol's new dim light. When he finished, he saw that Algol had dropped from the second magnitude to the fourth magnitude, a sixfold decrease in brightness. Like all astronomers, Goodricke kept a record of his observations. "I hardly believed it," he told people later.

The next day, Goodricke told Edward Pigott, the well-known astronomer, about his discovery. Pigott was Goodricke's neighbor and friend. Together, they had been studying the night sky, searching for clues about the stars, the planets, the galaxy, and the universe.

Goodricke and Pigott communicated by writing to each other with pencil and paper. Pigott did not use sign language and Goodricke, deaf since he was three months old, did not use his voice.

A Math Whiz

When he was very young, Goodricke attended the Braidwood School for the Deaf, a school in Scotland where deaf children learned to lipread and speak. Later, his parents sent him to a private school, the Warrington Academy. His parents may have felt nervous about sending their deaf son to a school with all hearing students and teachers, but they felt that it was necessary. Young John was the heir of his grandfather, Sir John Goodricke.

When he grew up, he would inherit a noble title and a lot of money. His parents wanted to make sure that their son was prepared.

They did not need to worry—at least not about John's grades. At Warrington Academy, John Goodricke did very well, especially in math. In fact, he became famous among the students and teachers for his math ability. He solved the hardest math problems with speed and skill.

Night after night, Pigott and Goodricke worked side by side.

When he returned to his home in York, Goodricke was 17 years old. He must have been delighted when Pigott, his neighbor, offered to teach him about astronomy. Student Goodricke quickly caught up with teacher Pigott. Despite their age difference, man and boy worked together night after night, side by side, as equals.

The Changing Light

Pigott was excited at Goodricke's discovery. The next night he joined Goodricke in another look at Algol. But that night Algol's light was no longer dim. Instead it was shining brightly. Goodricke stared. Perhaps he wondered again if his eyes had played tricks on him. Puzzled, he made another note in his journal—Algol was back to the second magnitude in brightness.

From then on, Goodricke pointed his telescope into the northern sky and measured the brightness of the fickle Algol every night. Finally on December 28, Goodricke saw Algol's light change again. Again it glimmered down to the fourth magnitude on the brightness scale. Goodricke was encouraged. He maintained his steady night watch.

After several weeks had passed, Goodricke realized that Algol became dim periodically. Using his math skill, Goodricke figured that Algol became dim every 2 days, 20 hours, and 45 minutes.

Pigott was thrilled. He wrote to all his famous friends in London about the discovery of "the deaf and dumb man." Then Goodricke wrote a paper for the Royal Society. The scientists met regularly and picked the best papers to read at their meetings. They picked Goodricke's paper.

In his paper, Goodricke wrote that Algol's brightness changed on a regular basis. He presented his measurements and his math. He also presented possible reasons why Algol's brightness changed.

"Perhaps it suffers an eclipse," he wrote. Perhaps there was another body—a planet or another star—circling Algol. If the circling body passed between Algol and the Earth, then Algol's brightness would change.

No one had ever written a paper about Algol. And the idea that stars might circle each other in the sky was a new one. The scientists were impressed. They liked Goodricke. They liked his math and they

Accepting the Copley Medal.

Shawn Richardson

liked his ideas. Goodricke became famous. He won the Copley Medal, a special medal for important astronomical discoveries, in 1783.

Goodricke wrote another paper on Algol. In his second paper, Goodricke wrote the exact measure of Algol's changes in brightness. Algol would be at its brightest every 2 days, 20 hours, 48 minutes, and 56 seconds. Goodricke's second calculation was within seconds of the modern measure.

On the strength of his fame, Goodricke journeyed to London to learn more about astronomy. All the famous scientists welcomed him. They wanted to help the young genius learn everything he could.

Then he returned to York to continue his search of the sky. He found two more stars like Algol—stars whose brightness varied. The stars were Betae Lyrae and Delta Cephei. Goodricke began to keep careful track. He measured their brightness almost every night.

Who knows how many other discoveries awaited the young astronomer? But Goodricke did not live to make them. On March 30, 1786, he measured Lyrae's brightness for the last time.

People thought he had a bad cold—probably from spending nights awake and working outside in the chilly air. If it was a cold, it got worse. By April 20, John Goodricke was dead. He was 21 years old.

In 1889, scientific techniques caught up with Goodricke. Scientists were able to prove that Algol was really two orbiting stars—a bright star and a dim star—just as Goodricke had predicted 100 years before.

Francisco Goya
1746-1828

After he became deaf,
Spain's top painter became a great artist.

Brush with Light

ON AN AFTERNOON in May, in 1808, people gathered along the sidewalk of a cafe near the center of Madrid, the largest city in the terrified country of Spain. In shock and horror, they tried to talk about what had happened the day before. Soldiers, sent to Spain by the dreaded Napoleon of France, had massacred everyone in their path. Men, women, and children had died—slaughtered by the French soldiers.

Suddenly a man broke from the crowd. The talking stopped as everyone turned to watch him. Everyone knew the man, of course. He was Francisco Goya, deaf and eccentric, and the most famous artist in Spain.

When he reached the street, Goya pulled his handkerchief from his coat pocket and dipped it in the mud. Suddenly the handkerchief became a paintbrush, the mud became paint, and the walls of the cafe became an enormous canvas. In bold strokes, Goya painted the massacre—soldiers firing and men, women and children falling dead. Again and again he returned to the street to dip his handkerchief in the mud. And again and again he returned to the wall, where he drew life-size people, and the act of agony and murder.

When he finished, the crowd was silent. All of the people stood in awe of his drawing. Goya, tired, but still filled with fevered energy, went to his studio and transformed his mud sketch into a painting. It was called *Le Tres de Mayo* or *The Third of May*, the date on which the massacre happened. It would become one of the most famous paintings in the world.

Young Rebel

It was not the first time Goya had used mud on walls to draw pictures. Goya was born outside the town of Zaragoza, the art capital of Aragon, a province of Spain. When he was a small boy, he often used mud and walls for paint and canvas. One day, a priest came by and saw one of his drawings. Some say it was a drawing of a pig; some say it was a drawing of a blind man.

"Come with me," the priest told the young boy. "And I will find you an art teacher."

The teacher was Don Jose Lugan, a kindly old man, who refused to take money for his work. But Goya's art lessons did not last long. He got into trouble with the law and ran away to Madrid.

Goya had a lot of energy, a hot temper, and a desire for many women. In Madrid, he got into trouble with the law again. Again he ran away. This time he fled through the countryside of southern Spain. Some people say that he paid for his trip by fighting bulls. He got on a boat and made his way to Rome. In Rome, Goya took a few art lessons, but mostly he played his guitar, chased after women, and challenged other young men to sword fights. He climbed the dome of the famous church, St. Peter, and carved his initials in its top.

Finally he returned to Spain. At age 25, he got a job drawing for the Royal Tapestry Works. He married Josefa Bayeu, whom he called "La Pepa."

Goya drew pictures of the court and famous people. Unlike some artists, he drew people who were not famous, too.

He met the king of Spain and asked to paint for the Royal Court. But twice the king refused to hire him. No one doubted his painting talent, but the Catholic Church, very powerful in Spain, remembered Goya's troubles as a young man. Further, Goya sometimes still got into trouble. He was rough with people; he did not try to make friends.

Some people were critical of Goya's art, as well. It was too much like real life, said some art critics. The critics preferred an older romantic style of painting that originated in Italy.

Playing Tricks

Goya, always full of tricks, thought of a plan to get back at his critics. First he asked a friend for help. Then he painted some pictures, copying the old Italian art style. Finally he asked the friend to hang the pictures in his home and invite one of the most famous critics to come look at them. "Pretend you discovered the pictures in Italy," Goya told his friend. "And ask the critic to write an article about them."

The plan worked as Goya had hoped. The critic loved the phony pictures. He wrote a long newspaper story praising the "old Italian paintings." Then Goya and his friend together published another newspaper story, explaining that the pictures were fakes painted by Goya himself. The critic was humiliated and Goya was triumphant.

Triumphant Artist

Goya was admitted to the Royal Academy of Fine Arts in 1786. It was about this time that he began to lose his hearing. People began to call him "semi-deaf."

Goya tried to ignore his hearing loss and enjoyed his life at the court. He continued to play tricks on people. When a noble lady asked him for help so she would not have to go on a trip with her husband, Goya was happy to paint a lifelike bruise on her ankle. When her husband saw it, he thought it was a real bruise and very kindly let his wife stay home.

When Goya was about 46 years old, he reached the height of his fame. He was frequently in the king's court, and his friends were the royal courtiers. One of his most famous friends was the Duchess of Alba.

Shawn Richardson

While lightning flashed, Goya painted.

A Deaf Man

Goya and the Duchess were travelling to one of her homes when a wheel broke on their carriage and Goya decided that he would repair the wheel himself. While the Duchess watched, Goya built a fire, and used the heat to reseal the break. Then the wheel was put back on the carriage and they were off.

A few days later, Goya caught a cold and blamed it on working on the wheel in the damp air. As usual, his ears seemed to fill up and he became deaf. At the Duchess's house, Goya waited to hear again.

Time passed. He was still deaf. Finally, Goya returned to his own home in a black mood. He was tired of waiting for his hearing to return. In frustration, he picked up his guitar and strummed it, but heard nothing. He clapped his hands near his ears, but he heard nothing. He pursed his lips and whistled, still nothing. Finally he gritted his teeth, rubbing his top teeth against his bottom teeth to see if he could hear something inside his head. Again, silence.

Outside a storm raged and Goya stared at the flashes of lightning that streaked the sky. Finally he turned to his wife. "Is there really no thunder?" he asked her.

"There's no thunder," his wife said. But Goya, looking at her face, knew she had lied. He turned from her in frustration. Then he grabbed his charcoal. He drew a face. He called it *Portrait of a Deaf Man*. It was a picture of himself.

A Great Artist

With this realization, Goya's art began to change. No longer was he satisfied painting cheerful court pictures. No longer did he paint only in bright colors. Deafness seemed to sharpen his eyesight, he told his friends. It helped him concentrate, too.

Goya continued to paint for the king, but his paintings were different now. His drawings were more creative. His portraits showed insight. People found parts of their characters, sometimes their very souls, reflected in Goya's paintings.

For example, in the painting *The Family of Charles IV*, Goya drew a king and queen who look foolish. The queen is located in the center of the painting, instead of the king, because Goya believed that she was the most important person in the royal family. The queen's face

Goya's famous painting, The Third of May, shows the massacre of innocent people.

is not beautiful and her expression looks silly. The king, painted toward the edge of the canvas, looks even more silly because Goya painted King Charles IV as a foolish man who was trying to look intelligent.

Goya's painting showed the suffering of his country. King Charles IV and his wife did not rule wisely and Spain's power declined. Perhaps that is partly why Goya's paintings became sad. During this time, he drew the devil eating his children and portrayed tormented people in the mental hospitals.

His personal life changed, too. He no longer cared about luxury. His wife worried because he slept on the floor or in a chair near the easel where he painted, instead of coming to bed.

When Goya came to court, the king and queen told him they were sorry that he was deaf. Of course they still wanted Goya to paint for them. In 1799, Goya became Chief Painter of the Chamber, the top position for the king's painter. The day of his appointment, King Charles IV asked him to ride with him in his personal carriage, an unequaled triumph for a painter. Afterward the king bragged that he and Goya conversed in sign language.

Goya used signs with everyone. He and his wife made up home signs. The sign for the Duchess of Alba was a hand motion showing her wavy hair. Goya learned how to make the letters of the alphabet with his fingers. His finger alphabet was probably an ancestor of the same finger alphabet that is used by Spanish, French, and American deaf people today.

The Metropolitan Museum of Art

One of Goya's many self portraits.

He taught the alphabet to Leocadia Zorrilla, a woman who became his friend. Perhaps he was surprised at the words that flew from Zorrilla's fingers. "Spain is a poor and evil country," she said. "Napoleon will conquer us—and he should." Goya burst out laughing. He wasn't used to women thinking about politics.

Zorrilla's prediction was right. Napoleon came, saw, conquered, and gave the Spanish crown to his younger brother, Joseph. Goya kept painting. Joseph Napoleon governed for five years and Goya painted for his court. Then the Spanish forced Napoleon out of their country and a republican government came to power. Goya painted for the republicans, too. Soon the royalists overthrew the republicans, and King Ferdinand VII, son of King Charles IV, ascended to the Spanish throne. King Ferdinand killed and imprisoned most republicans and the people who worked for them.

Goya, he pardoned. Goya was growing old as the king's chief painter. Finally he retired at age 74, moving to a country house outside of Madrid. "Huerto del sordo," everyone called it, "house of the deaf man." Still he kept painting.

At 77, Goya found himself in trouble again. Some people were mad that the king had pardoned Goya. They told the king that he should punish Goya for painting for Napoleon and the republicans. Other people told the king that he should punish Goya for painting a naked lady. Both actions were crimes and punishable by death.

Goya's friends pleaded with the king not to kill the old painter. But Goya was not taking any chances. He fled. His eyes were failing and he was weak, but he traveled alone, crossing the mountains at the Spanish border and moving into a town in southern France. His neighbors called him "the deaf old lion." He made his last drawings in France, a series of lithographs.

Goya was not one great artist, he was 20 great artists, a famous French art critic wrote. When he returned to Spain to die in 1828, the world of art was changed forever.

John Robert Gregg
1867-1948

He arrived in the United States with $130 in his pocket,
but he was about to succeed in his lifelong goal,
leaving a new system of writing that all the world would use.

Writing for the World

JOHN ROBERT GREGG, the youngest child in his family, hated the school in his hometown of Rockcorry, Ireland. The students called him "stupid" and the teachers called him "slow." When every child in the class got a number showing where they stood in their class, John Gregg got the last number. He was at the bottom of his class! To make matters worse, all of his brothers and sisters were very smart, especially Franny and George, who took home all the school prizes. Everyone said Franny and George were brilliant.

John's father scolded his "stupid" son and tried to make him study. His teacher hit him with a cane and made fun of him in front of the other students. Once the teacher even boxed his ears. But John was not stupid, he just could not hear well. How could he understand what the teacher said when he could not hear well?

One day, a visitor to the Gregg home attended church with the family. During the service, the visitor wrote the entire sermon in a strange script called shorthand. The Gregg family had never heard of shorthand. Neither had anyone else in town. When the preacher saw that the visitor had written down his sermon word for word, he was horrified. "Don't publish it," he insisted. "It is my sermon, not yours."

John's father was fascinated. Here was a new system of writing that his children should learn. He found some books on shorthand and encouraged his children to make the strange letters. Franny and George were confused by it. Only John learned it well. In fact, after John learned one shorthand system, he found a book on another shorthand system and learned that one too.

John even tried to improve the shorthand systems. He looked for simpler ways to write letters and quicker ways to join them together. He wanted to make shorthand faster and more efficient.

When John Gregg turned 18, he graduated from high school and got a job as a clerk for a lawyer. The lawyer was often drunk so Gregg had lots of free time. He used his time to study shorthand and learn several different systems of writing it. He corresponded with the inventors of shorthand in England, France, and Germany.

John began to work on his own shorthand system too, trying to make it perfect. With Gregg's improved shorthand, he could write more and he could write faster.

Then Gregg met a man named Malone. Malone was a hearing man who was much older than Gregg and owned a shorthand school. Malone hired Gregg as a teacher and the two men talked often about Gregg's new shorthand. "Let's write a book," Malone suggested.

Gregg was enthusiastic. The two men wrote the book together. It showed all Gregg's improvements. The book was called Script Phonography.

When he saw the new book, Gregg was disappointed and angry. His name was not on the book! Only Malone's name appeared.

Gregg watched, amazed and intrigued, as the visitor jotted down the sermon in shorthand.

Who would know that he was an author, too? No one! Who would know that all the improvements in shorthand came from him? No one.

When the book started to make a little money, Malone took it all. Gregg felt cheated and betrayed. He could barely afford to eat or pay his rent. Every day, he struggled against poverty. He kept his anger private. He kept working on his shorthand, too, practicing and trying to find ways to make his system faster.

Then he learned bad news. His sister, Franny, was dying and his brother, George, was already dead. Both were victims of tuberculosis. In grief and shock, Gregg stopped working. He put all his shorthand notes into a brown parcel and closed it up. After a few weeks, he left town.

He went to Liverpool, England, and joined his brother Samuel. Gregg had saved a little money and he used it to set up a little shop. It was on the 10th floor and few customers would bother to climb the narrow dark staircase, but he didn't care.

Shorthand Inventor

After several months in Liverpool, Gregg unwrapped his parcel. Nervously, he looked at his old notes. Suddenly he realized that his notes were much better than he thought. In fact, his notes were really a book. Once published, the book would show a whole new way, a much better way, to write shorthand. The new shorthand "was easy to write and beautiful to look at," said Gregg.

Gregg taught his student shorthand.

He went to his brother Samuel, and asked to borrow money to publish his book. Samuel laughed. "You are wasting your time on this idiotic shorthand," Samuel told Gregg. "Why don't you make a living at something sensible?" Gregg could not accept his brother's opinion and continued to beg him for money to publish his book. Finally his brother loaned him 10 pounds. "I'll never see that money again," Samuel grumbled.

Excited, Gregg hunted for a cheap printer and printed 500 copies of his small 28-page book. After it was printed, Gregg publicly challenged people to try his new system. He showed how fast he could copy speeches from newspapers. He taught other people to use his shorthand and dared them to compete in contests against other shorthand users. He began to write for two shorthand magazines.

In the middle of his work, Gregg's hearing disappeared completely. Used to being hard-of-hearing, Gregg was shocked to be totally deaf. He stopped teaching. He stopped lecturing. He became isolated. After six months, he moved again. This time, he sailed to America.

In America

Gregg arrived in Boston with 130 dollars in his pocket. He met one of his former students and the two men opened a shorthand school together. The school had one desk, which they shared to train two students at a time.

Their reputation grew. Soon Gregg took a job teaching at the Boys Institute of Industry. With his former student, Gregg produced his first American book. However, he continued to struggle with money. He told people that he would return to England, if he could afford it.

After two years, he left Boston, travelling alone to Chicago. With 75 dollars in his pocket, he looked for the cheapest place he could find, rented it, and bought furniture. He was still polishing the furniture when his first customer arrived.

Gregg's shorthand school grew slowly but steadily. Just when Gregg was starting to feel successful again, fire struck. As his office was engulfed in smoke and flames, Gregg jumped out the window. He was safe, but he had lost everything. Convinced his shorthand was the best in the world, he opened another school almost immediately. This time nothing would stop him. Previously, most of his students were male, but now women, moving from farms to city and getting office jobs, were learning shorthand, too. High schools even began to require that students take shorthand. It was the dawn of a new age.

Gregg's students entered the World Championship in Shorthand. They won it a total of six times. Some of them became famous. One became the personal secretary to President Woodrow Wilson; another was offered a job at the Supreme Court.

In 1927, Martin Dupraw won the World Shorthand Championship using Gregg shorthand, writing an astounding 282 words per minute for five minutes, a rate that is twice as fast as people talk. To this day, no one has equaled Dupraw's score.

Gregg shorthand and its inventor were famous. In addition to thousands of books in the United States and England, Gregg published books in Poland, Italy, and Spain.

As he grew older, Gregg was awarded honorary degrees, a Master's of Commercial Science, and a Doctorate of Commercial Education. He traveled often and donated much of his money to charity.

When he collapsed and died at 81 years old in 1948, Gregg shorthand had become the worldwide standard—and it remains so to this day.

James Howe
1780-1836

He begin drawing in margins and on scrap paper and
went on to become Scotland's first animal painter.

Painting the Animals

IN 1815, WHEN the British finally defeated Napoleon at Waterloo, they needed a painter to immortalize the great battle. They decided to hire James Howe, Scotland's famous artist, who had been deaf as long as anyone could remember. Howe visited the battlefield where so many men had died, and painted the battle scene vividly on a huge canvas. Today it is one of his most famous paintings.

Howe always loved to draw. When he was a little boy, he drew on every piece of paper he could find. Sometimes when his father, a minister, pulled out his papers to read his sermons at church on Sunday morning, he found James's drawings decorating the edges of his papers.

James drew everything—people, flowers, tools. But mostly he drew animals. He tried to go to school. For a while, he went to the village school in Skirling, near his home, but he quit when he was still young. He was deaf and could not understand his teacher or the other students in the small class.

At 14, he got his first opportunity to paint for money. He joined a group of house painters as an apprentice. But Howe preferred artistic painting. He quit painting houses and began to paint portraits. Finally he set up his own studio.

As a child, James Howe drew on all the paper he could find.

Shawn Richardson

When Howe hung drawings of animals in his window, his business grew.

Then one day he painted a pony and hung it in his window. People were fascinated with the painting. The pony looked so real, almost as if it were alive. People began to ask Howe to paint other animals. Britain's Board of Agriculture asked him to paint different breeds of cattle.

When Howe died in 1836, he was famous as Scotland's first and perhaps its greatest animal painter.

National Baseball Hall of Fame

William Hoy
1862-1961

This no-nonsense ballplayer brought the signals
to baseball that people still use today.

Tops in His Field

IN THE LATE 1800s, a young graduate of the Ohio School for the Deaf showed up to play baseball for his neighborhood team. He was five-foot-five inches tall and weighed 148 pounds. He flashed around the field with the speed of lightning and he hit well, too.

One day, a stranger passed by and watched the gifted ball player. He wanted that man for his own hometown team! As the stranger approached the ballplayer, he realized that the ballplayer couldn't hear. Having no idea how to talk with a deaf man, he gave up and turned away.

Fortunately for baseball—and the man's hometown team—he returned the next day. He conquered his shyness and asked the deaf man to play for his team, the Kenton team, in its game against the Urbana team. Urbana had recently hired a professional pitcher, the stranger explained, and the Kenton team was nervous about playing against him.

The man accepted the stranger's proposal. He joined Kenton in its game against Urbana, and he played exceptionally well, hitting three singles and a home run. As the crowd roared its approval, William Hoy realized that he could make baseball a career.

A few days later, Hoy hammered out spikes from a steel saw and made himself a pair of baseball shoes. He hung a "Shop Closed" sign in his cobbler shop window and left town. He walked out in the middle of the night. He did not dare to tell his parents where he was going.

He was going to become a baseball star.

Signs from Ohio

William Hoy became deaf from an illness, probably meningitis, when he was two or three years old. He stayed at home until he was 10 years old, when his parents learned about the Ohio School for the Deaf (OSD) and sent their son there. Hoy did well at OSD. He finished 12 years of school in eight years and graduated at the top of his class.

At OSD, Hoy learned to read, write, and play baseball. OSD had a strong baseball tradition. Edward Joseph "Dummy" Dundon, the first deaf major leaguer, was an OSD graduate. Perhaps partly because of its enthusiasm and strong tradition, OSD had devised a system of hand signals to use during games that let deaf players and fans know if the pitches were balls or strikes.

When Hoy graduated, he returned to Houcktown, his small hometown, to become a cobbler. He worked with an older man and eventually took over his business repairing shoes. Even as he left his home to go play baseball, Hoy planned to cut short his baseball season and return to fill his shoe orders.

When Hoy arrived at the Milwaukee ballpark, he wrote his request for a chance to play ball and passed it to the team's manager. The manager laughed at him, but Hoy persisted. Finally the manager let him try out. When he saw Hoy's skills, the manager was surprised. He asked Hoy how much money he wanted to play for his team. "Seventy-five dollars a month," said Hoy. The manager thought he could save money. "Sixty dollars," he offered.

Hoy shook his head and traveled on. He arrived in Oshkosh, Wisconsin, and again approached its baseball team manager. Again he wrote a note asking for a tryout. The manager, Frank Selee, agreed to watch him play.

Like the manager from Milwaukee, Selee was impressed. "How much money do you want?" he asked Hoy. "Seventy-five dollars a month," Hoy said again. "You got it!" said Selee.

As soon as Hoy accepted the Oshkosh offer, the captain from the Milwaukee team showed up. When he learned that Oshkosh had met Hoy's request for seventy-five dollars a month, he offered to pay him eighty-five dollars a month.

"I wouldn't play for you for a million dollars," said Hoy.

New Name

It was probably while he was playing for Oshkosh that Hoy got his nickname "Dummy," the same nickname that major leaguer and fellow OSD graduate Edward Dundon had earned. Hoy rather liked his nickname. When he signed autographs, he abbreviated his first name as "Wm.," used "E." for his middle initial, and wrote his last name "Hoy." After that, he always added "D-M" for deaf mute.

One day a reporter came to interview the Oshkosh team. He asked all the team members, except Hoy, their ages. The reporter avoided

Hoy asked for the job by writing notes to the manager.

Shawn Richardson

talking with Hoy. Like the first manager, he was too shy or too impatient to try to talk with a deaf man. Instead the reporter guessed Hoy's age. He guessed wrong. Hoy was already 24 years old and the reporter guessed his age at 20. The mistake led to confusion about Hoy's age for many years.

Hoy never returned to work in his cobbler shop. He did go back home to visit his parents, and they forgave him for his midnight flight months before. Meanwhile Oshkosh doubled his salary to make sure that he played for their team for the full season.

At bat, Hoy had a difficult time learning his own ball/strike count. Usually he guessed, but guessing was unreliable and stressful. Finally Hoy asked the third base coach to flash him the signals he had used at OSD. The count for strikes was shown on the right hand; for balls, on the left hand.

Slowly the umpires picked up the signals, too. It became clear that hand signals were helpful for the hearing audience as well as the deaf ballplayer, especially if there was a large crowd.

In the Baseball Hall of Fame, other umpires are credited with inventing these hand signals, which are the same ones in use today. But they did not work until 1904–1905, and Hoy was teaching major league coaches, umps, and players the signs in 1891, more than 10 years before!

Major Leaguer

After two years of playing for Oshkosh, Hoy moved on. He joined the Washington Senators and became a Major League ballplayer.

Hoy always carried a pen and note pad in his shirt pocket to communicate with hearing people. When he disagreed with the umpires, he would write polite notes challenging them.

Teaching an umpire the sign STRIKE.

In the rough and tumble days of early baseball, when fights broke out often between players and umpires, Hoy was a gentleman.

The first year that Hoy played with the Senators, he had to teach the team what it was like to play ball with a deaf teammate. Teaching them the signals was the easy part. Once, the Senators planned to play an exhibition game in New Jersey on an off-day. But the manager forgot to tell Hoy. When the team got together to make the journey to the ballpark, Hoy was missing.

His teammates found Hoy fast asleep in his hotel room—a normal place for a man to be if he didn't know he had a morning baseball game. The hearing men pounded on the door and screamed, but of course, Hoy slept on. The whole team gathered to discuss the dilemma. A bellboy tried to squeeze through a space at the top of the door, but could not quite fit. Someone threw a plug of tobacco through the same space. It hit Hoy on the shoulder, but he didn't budge. Then they threw cards toward his sleeping body. Some circled and landed near his face, but none woke him.

Finally a bed sheet was tied to a large key ring filled with keys. The men hurled the keys into the bedroom, then pulled them back toward their position on the other side of the door. One of the keys caught on Hoy's pajamas. The men

Hoy, a baseball legend, once threw three people out at home plate in one game.

National Baseball Hall of Fame

tugged and tugged. Finally Hoy opened his eyes. He reacted angrily, seizing a nearby pitcher of water and hurling it toward his astounded tormentors.

The teammates explained the problem and Hoy hurried to get dressed and play ball. But after that experience, the managers made sure Hoy knew about games that were not listed on the schedule.

Hoy said that his deafness was not a problem on the ball field. It helped him concentrate, he said. He was not upset when people booed, nor distracted when they cheered.

In 1898, Hoy married Anna Maria Lowery. Anna's mother had died when she was a little girl and she had grown up in an orphanage, the "Children's Home." Deaf like her husband, Anna was a graduate of a Cincinnati oral school. She once called herself "the third best lipreader in America," though to this day, no one knows whom she considered lipreaders one and two.

It was no easy job for Hoy to win Anna's hand in marriage. In those days, playing baseball was not considered a respectable occupation. Anna's guardians investigated Hoy thoroughly before they would let the young girl marry him.

"He came forth with flying colors," they reported, ". . . a man of honor and high moral character, whose leisure was spent in reading."

The two were married in the "biggest and brightest wedding" ever conducted at the Children's Home, people said. Hoy and his wife had three children, two of whom became teachers at the state school for the deaf.

Many of Hoy's feats are still remembered. Once he caught a fly ball in fog so thick that no one could see the ball until he held up his glove. Another time he dashed onto one of the carriages that had pulled up near the ballpark and stood on it to catch a fly ball. He hit the second grand-slam home run in the American League. Hoy himself said his best memory was the time he threw three people out at home in one game, a record that still stands today.

Once when the Senators faced the New York Giants, Hoy faced another deaf major leaguer, Luther Haden Taylor. Taylor was pitching when Hoy came to bat, marking the only time in history that two deaf ball players faced each other as pitcher and batter in the major leagues.

According to the newspapers, Hoy signed to Taylor, "I'm glad to see you," then slammed the ball to center field. Taylor made sure that Hoy didn't steal any bases, but Hoy got one run and two hits off him. The Giants won 5 to 3, with all five runs in the ninth inning.

In 1894, Hoy was sold to the Cincinnati Reds. He liked Cincinnati so much he moved his family there. When he retired from baseball, he had played 1,795 games in a 15-year career. He had hit 41 home runs, stolen 600 bases, and was considered one of the best outfielders in baseball.

Courtesy of Steven R. Sandy

A spry 99-year-old Hoy throws out the first ball to begin the 1961 Reds—Cubs game.

Although he hated lipreading and loved sign language, Hoy earned a reputation on the team as a lipreader. Opposing players sometimes hid their mouths from him when they planned their strategy.

He lived to be 99 years old, still hopping the bus to ride to baseball games. When he threw out the ceremonial first ball of the 1961 Reds-Cubs game, reporters said that he showed the zest of a teenager. He died soon after, and was eulogized in newspapers by sports writers around the country.

Gallaudet University Archives

Helen Keller
1880-1968

*From the time she was a little girl, she devoted
her life to helping other deaf and blind people.*

A Life of Helping Others

IT WAS 1891, and 11-year-old Helen Keller had just finished her speech lesson. Wearily, she sat down. Anne Sullivan, the woman Helen called "Teacher," began to spell in her hand.

Using the finger alphabet to spell out what she said, Sullivan told Helen about a young boy named Tommy Stringer. Tommy was five years old and deaf and blind. His mother was dead and his father could not take care of him.

"Tommy has been taken to the poor house," said Sullivan. "A terrible place for a little boy."

Helen Keller knew that Sullivan had also been in a poor house when she was a little girl. She knew that her teacher was upset to think about a little boy suffering as she herself had suffered.

"Can't Tommy come here?" Helen asked.

"Here" was Perkins Institution for the Blind, in Boston, Massachusetts, where Helen was taught privately by Sullivan. Helen and Sullivan worked together, as they had since they had met each other in Helen's home four years before; Helen was the only student in the school who was deaf as well as blind and the other teachers could not easily communicate with her.

"Can't Tommy get a teacher, too?" Helen persisted.

Anne Sullivan shook her head. Not all deaf and blind children were as lucky as Helen. "It takes money," said Sullivan.

"Well, let's get some money," replied Helen.

And she did.

Helen Keller sat down at the typewriter and wrote letters to everyone she knew, asking them to send money to help Tommy Stringer. She also decided to use her own money that people had previously sent to her for her education. People responded to Helen's request. Before long, there was enough money to bring Tommy Stringer to Perkins Institution and get him a teacher.

It was the first time that Helen Keller had raised money to help another deaf and blind person. She did not know it, but at 11 years old she had discovered her life's work.

Everything Has a Name

Helen Keller lost her sight and her hearing from illness when she was two years old. Her parents wanted the best for their little daughter, but they had no idea how to communicate with a child who was deaf and blind. By the time Helen was seven years old, she cried often and threw temper tantrums. Once she even threatened to hurt her little sister.

Finally Helen's doctor recommended that her parents write to Alexander Graham Bell, the famous inventor of the telephone and a teacher of the deaf. Perhaps Bell could help them with their daughter.

After he received their letter, Bell suggested that they contact the Perkins Institution for the Blind. They did, and the school sent a special teacher to the Keller home. The teacher was Anne Sullivan, 20 years old, and excited to teach her first child.

Sullivan was amazed at how quickly Helen learned to fingerspell. Helen learned the handshapes with ease and soon she could spell many words. But Helen's father was not impressed. Yes, Helen had learned to fingerspell words, he admitted, but she did not know what the words meant. Fingerspelling was just a game to her.

Helen's father was right. Helen knew that when she made different shapes with her hands she was praised. Other people knew that the shapes represented letters, such as *D, L, O, or G,* and that the letters spelled words, such as "dog" or "doll." But for Helen, fingerspelling was just fun that she had with the stranger who had come to her parents' house and tried to force her to behave.

One day Helen threw a terrible temper tantrum. In anger, she threw her doll to the floor and its head broke. As she felt the pieces of the head with her hands, she was too angry to be sorry.

Sullivan was angry, too. It seemed Helen would never learn to behave properly. Sullivan led Helen out to the water pump to get some water. She gave Helen a cup and pumped the water. By habit, she fingerspelled into Helen's hands. "W-A-T-E-R," she spelled, as the water flowed.

Suddenly Helen dropped the cup.

Sullivan may have been annoyed at first—then she saw Helen's face. Helen was staring upward, her whole body stiff, as if she were afraid to breathe. Then she groped for Sullivan's hand.

"W-A-T-E-R," she spelled back.

Not quite believing what was happening, Sullivan patted Helen's back, to indicate that she was right. Helen stretched one hand to the ground, keeping her other hand in Sullivan's.

"What's that?" she was asking.

"G-R-O-U-N-D,"responded Sullivan.

"And that?" Now her hand was on the pump.

"P-U-M-P."

"And that?"

"V-I-N-E."

Sullivan spelled everything as fast as she could in Helen's hands. Helen led Sullivan back inside the house, grasping the skirt of her surprised nurse, then touching her little sister in the nurse's arms. "N-U-R-S-E," spelled Sullivan, trying to keep up with her excited student. "B-A-B-Y." Then Helen asked about her mother and Sullivan. Finally, she asked about herself.

"H-E-L-E-N K-E-L-L-E-R," Sullivan told her.

For the first time, Helen knew her own name and the names that filled her household. After that, no one doubted that she could learn. Even her father was excited. Captain Keller sat down and learned fingerspelling so that he could communicate with his daughter.

From names, Sullivan moved on to help Helen form sentences. Then she taught her Braille. By the time Tommy's letter arrived, Helen could write in two ways. She wrote Braille for her blind friends; she typed on a typewriter for those who could see.

By this time, Helen had become famous too. When her dog died, many people sent her money to buy a new dog. Helen Keller used it to help Tommy Stringer.

Gallaudet University Archives

As a young girl, Helen talked in fingerspelling with the man who had helped her find a teacher, Alexander Graham Bell.

College Girl

Even Anne Sullivan was surprised when Helen told her that she wanted to go to Radcliffe. Radcliffe was the top college for women in the United States and many very smart students were refused admission. But Sullivan would never have discouraged her student.

So she and Keller began to prepare for the entrance exam. Student and teacher worked hard every day preparing for the examination. When no Braille books were available, Sullivan would read printed books and interpret every page into Keller's palm.

Finally came the day of the examination. Sullivan was not permitted to interpret for Keller, and she had to find another interpreter. It didn't matter. Keller passed everything.

Still Radcliffe refused to accept her. Radcliffe's professors said that they did not believe a deaf-blind student could keep up with the hearing-sighted students.

Keller ignored their decision. Officials at other top schools, Cornell and the University of Chicago, said that they would accept her. But Keller refused. Weeks passed.

Finally Keller sat down and wrote a letter. "A true soldier does not admit defeat before the battle," she told Radcliffe's professors and admitting officials. A day or two after Radcliffe's fall semester had begun, the school finally accepted her. Helen Keller became a freshman and was elected vice president of the student body government.

While Helen was a college student, Sullivan's eyesight grew worse. Sometimes the two women had to find other people to interpret for Helen.

Keller faced a special struggle in her English class. Even though she tried very hard, sometimes rewriting her papers many times, she never got good grades for writing. Finally her English teacher took her aside. While Sullivan interpreted, the teacher told Keller that she was trying to write like students who could hear and see.

"Write about what you know," he told her. "Write about your own experience."

Keller paid attention to the advice. She began to express herself instead of trying to copy other people. In fact, her writing became so good that people offered to publish it. With the help of a Harvard teacher, she began writing a book about herself. *The Story of My Life* became a best-seller.

The Real World

After college Helen Keller faced the same problem many college graduates face. How would she earn her living? As Keller grew up and Sullivan grew old, Keller began to feel that she should earn enough money to support both of them.

At first, she thought she could write books. She tried writing articles about eye care and blindness, but no one bought them. A rich American offered to put her on a pension and send her money every month. At first she said no. But as Keller and Sullivan faced poverty, Keller changed her mind and accepted money from her patron.

Helen Keller, relaxing at home.

Then she accepted another offer to earn money. In exchange for a fee, Keller began giving speeches about her own life. She went on stage, used her voice, and talked to her audience. No stranger could understand Keller's voice. So Sullivan, who hated crowds and bright lights, faced the audiences, too—and repeated everything Keller said.

Together, Keller and Sullivan began to earn large sums of money.

Of course Keller never planned to use the money for herself. By this time, she was working for the American Foundation for the Blind. Most of her money went to support that organization and help blind people.

Keller started the Helen Keller Endowment fund with $2 million that she raised from her friends. During World War II, she helped blind soldiers. She lectured in 25 countries and traveled around the world.

Sullivan's Influence

Sullivan was Keller's first teacher and the role model of her youth. When she was a little girl, Helen had learned everything about the world from Braille books or Sullivan's fingers. Through Sullivan, Keller learned Tadoma, the difficult art of lipreading people by placing one hand on their throat and the other on their lips.

Sullivan did not know much about deaf people or the deaf community. She herself had been blind when she was a little girl and her eyes were still very weak. So it would have been natural for Sullivan to train Helen to identify with blind people, not deaf people. Once, Helen met Laura Bridgeman, a deaf-blind woman, but Bridgeman was much older than Helen and they did not establish a close relationship.

Perhaps as a result, Keller told people she would rather be blind than deaf. "Blindness cuts you off from things, deafness cuts you off from people," Keller said. But she never really knew deaf people, or what being deaf could mean.

Anne Sullivan died in 1936 at the age of 70, and a young woman, Polly Thompson, came to work for Keller. Helen Keller continued working until her death in 1968. She was 88 years old.

Today the Helen Keller Center in New York continues to bring help to deaf and blind people throughout the world.

Courtesy of Girl Scouts of America

Juliette "Daisy" Gordon Low
1860-1927

With guts and good will, Juliette Gordon Low
founded the Girl Scouts in America.

The Best Scout

IN 1879, JULIETTE Gordon went to her hometown doctor in Savannah, Georgia. She told him that her ears hurt and she could no longer hear well. She told him that he would cure her and she told him how he would do it!

The doctor hesitated. He was not used to patients telling him what to do. But Juliette Gordon, the young woman everyone called "Daisy," was outspoken and stubborn. She was also used to seeing something before everyone else saw it, and used to getting her own way.

Daisy explained to the doctor that she had just returned from New York City, where she had learned that doctors had a new medicine to make deaf and hard-of-hearing people hear better. The new medicine was silver nitrate, a drug that doctors had used for many years, but that had only recently been used as a cure for deafness.

Daisy insisted that the doctor administer silver nitrate to help her hear again. Perhaps she was too persuasive for her own good. Finally the doctor got a vial of silver nitrate and worked it into her ears.

Daisy was not prepared for the pain. It seared through her head and made her dizzy and sick to her stomach. Determined to hide her suffering, she stumbled to her feet, thanked the doctor, and left.

When she got home, she collapsed in bed. Alarmed, her family called the doctor again. The family told him to come see their daughter at home, and bring another doctor with him.

The two doctors came to the Gordon house immediately, but there was nothing they could do to help Daisy. She remained sick for a long time. Afterward, she was completely deaf. She went to many doctors, but there was nothing anyone could do. She would always blame her deafness on silver nitrate, the famous cure for deafness that spread around the world in the 1800s. It did nothing except perhaps cause a lot of pain for deaf patients and sometimes make them more deaf.

Spunky Southern Daughter

When Daisy was only six years old, her mother brought her into the family living room to meet General Sherman, who had invaded her Georgia homeland with his Yankee Army. As the daughter of a Southern army colonel, Daisy was expected to be nervous and quiet in front of Sherman. She wasn't. She was only curious. When she noticed one of Sherman's soldiers had only one arm, she told him that it was probably her father who had shot off his other arm. "My daddy has shot lots of Yankees," she told him matter of factly. No one knows how Sherman felt. But Daisy's mother was horrified. She ushered her little girl quickly out of the room.

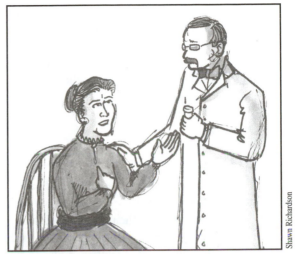

She insisted that the doctor give her the medicine.

Although Daisy got good grades at school, she was often in trouble there. She liked to draw and she angered her teachers by drawing all the time. In school, all the students were supposed to talk in French or German, but Daisy thought that rule was silly. She continued to talk to her friends in English.

Daisy's independent spirit showed again when she picked a husband. She picked William Low, a wealthy Englishman. Her father did not like him, but Daisy married him anyway.

English Wife

As the wife of William Low, Daisy Gordon Low became part of England's rich and noble class. She partied with her neighbors—the Prince of Wales and the Earl of Warwick. She was presented to the queen. Her life seemed perfect. But it wasn't.

Her husband lived up to her father's worst fears. He drank too much and he was often not home. When he did come home, he was cruel. Sometimes he teased his wife because she was deaf. He would turn from her so she could not see his lips and he would speak so quickly that she could not possibly understand him.

Despite her unhappiness, Daisy Low sought ways to try to help other people. When the Spanish-American War broke out, she came home to Georgia. She worked in a hospital in Savannah, nursing the men who were hurt in the war.

In the hospital, she showed that her creativity was as strong as her good will and stubbornness. When the men learned that due to the food shortage and their own weak condition, they were being fed baby food, they refused to eat it. The nurses and doctors were upset. If the sick men refused food, how could they become well?

Daisy Low solved the problem: She brought a bottle of rum into the hospital ward. While the men watched, she added a little rum to each dish of baby food. "It's adult food now," she told her patients, smiling. The men agreed. They ate it all.

When Low returned to England, sadness awaited her. William Low brought a strange woman into their home. He treated the woman as if she were his wife.

Daisy Low was horrified. She got a lawyer and filed for divorce, but in those days, divorce was a slow and difficult process. Finally in 1905, William Low died, leaving Daisy Low a widow.

Starting Scouts

Six years later, Low had the conversation that changed her life—and the lives of thousands of American girls. She was enjoying a dinner with Sir Robert Baden-Powell and his sister, Lady Agnes, at their home in England. Sir Robert told her about a new organization that he had started for English boys. It was called the Boy Scouts and its purpose was to help boys learn to think independently and live on their own, especially in the woods. His sister, Lady Agnes, had started a similar organization for English girls.

Low was thrilled. She wanted to become a troop leader and have her own troop of girls. The Baden-Powells enthusiastically agreed. Soon Low had all the girls in her neighborhood over for tea. They decided to form a troop and Low became their leader.

Gallaudet University Archives

Low in uniform.

The girls learned how to cook, garden, and raise animals. Low found a way for them to earn money by raising and selling chickens. Then Low told the Baden-Powells she wanted to bring scouting to America. Again, they were enthusiastic. Who could be better than Daisy Gordon Low to bring girl scouting to the United States?

But when Low arrived in Savannah and told her own family of her plans, her mother was doubtful. How could a deaf woman start an organization, her mother wondered? Fortunately, she tried to keep her doubts to herself.

Low, for her part, had already learned to use her deafness in a positive way. When she asked a friend to take over her English troop so that she could come to America, her friend said "No." But Low pretended not to understand her. "Thank you very much," she replied. The woman became an instant troop leader!

In 1912, Low started a Girl Scout troop in the United States. By 1913, she had established a national headquarters in Washington, D.C. Low visited the White House and received support from President Woodrow Wilson and his wife.

In England, the girls were called "Girl Guides" instead of "Girl Scouts." Low felt that in America, the girls' and boys' scouting organizations should have the same name.

The Girl Scouts of America continued to grow. In 1914, when World War I broke out, Low sold her pearls to raise money to keep the scouts going. "Scouting is patriotic," she often said.

The Girl Scouts began to have regular worldwide meetings and in 1926, Low arranged to bring the third

Today there are about 3 million Girl Scouts in America.

international Girl Scout meeting to America. Girl Scouts came from China, Egypt, England, and many other countries. Low was honored as the Founder of the American Girl Scouts.

She told almost no one at the meeting, but she was very sick. She had cancer. As Low celebrated with Girl Scouts from around the world, she knew that soon she would die.

A year later, Juliette Gordon Low was buried. She wore her Girl Scout uniform with a note from a friend in her uniform pocket: "You are the best Girl Scout of all," it said. She was 67 years old. Low left behind 167,000 American Girl Scouts. Today there are about 3 million.

Francis Humberstone MacKenzie
Sixth Lord Seaforth
1754-1815

Born deaf, this British nobleman taught his friends fingerspelling, raised an army, and became a member of Parliament and governor of Barbados.

Helping Britain Rule

NO ONE EXPECTED him to win, but Francis Humberstone MacKenzie was running for Parliament. It was 1784 and Scottish clan loyalty was very strong. MacKenzie—"Lord MacKenzie," the British called him—was determined to replace Lord McLeod. If he won the election, Lord MacKenzie would help the British rule a growing empire.

MacKenzie had become chief of the noble MacKenzie clan in 1781. Everyone knew him. To talk to him, they used fingerspelling, as MacKenzie had been deaf since birth.

Teaching Fingerspelling to All

When he was a little boy, MacKenzie went to an oral school in Edinburgh. He learned to speak a little bit, but he much preferred to talk with his friends using signs and fingerspelling. He taught all the hearing people he knew the finger alphabet and they often used it to converse with him.

One day he was invited to the house of Lord and Lady Melville for a dinner party. Before MacKenzie arrived, two of Lady Melville's guests entered the home and met each other just outside of the dining room. Having learned that there was a deaf dinner guest, each assumed the other was the deaf guest. They sat down and started talking to each other in fingerspelling.

When Lady Melville walked in and saw her hearing friends fingerspelling with each other, she burst out laughing.

"I thought you were deaf," each surprised guest told the other. The moment ended with lots of laughter. When MacKenzie arrived, he had quite a laugh too.

Shawn Richardson

When he arrived, he saw two guests fingerspelling to each other.

90

MacKenzie wrote many letters to friends who lived far away. The letters, friendly and articulate, have been preserved to this day.

When the election was over, MacKenzie was declared the winner. He probably became the first deaf individual to win an elective office, and he was just beginning his career.

MacKenzie won a seat in Parliament.

War with France

MacKenzie served in Parliament until 1790. Then he retired and returned home to earn money.

When war broke out against France, MacKenzie raised an army of soldiers in his Scottish homeland. They formed the 78th Regiment of Foot, Ross-Shire Militia. MacKenzie himself was the Lieutenant-Colonel Commanding. In 1794, he added another battalion of soldiers. In 1808, he rose to the rank of Lieutenant General. He ran for Parliament again and was re-elected by a large margin. When he returned to Parliament, he gave strong support to the government.In appreciation, the government named him the Sixth Lord of Seaforth.

In 1808, MacKenzie, now the Sixth Lord Seaforth, became governor of Barbados. He served there for several years. He is known for trying to improve the conditions of the slaves.

Afterward, he returned to Britain. Sadly, he ran out of money and had to sell his house and much of his land. He had a wife, four sons and six daughters. MacKenzie died in 1814.

Antonio Magarotto
1891-1966

First he helped organize deaf people in Italy,
then he helped deaf people organize around the world.

Brave Founder

IT WAS 1932, and a deaf man stood before Benito Mussolini, the fascist dictator who murdered thousands of his countrymen and helped to start World War II. The deaf man was Antonio Magarotto—and he had a complaint.

Using one of his young hearing sons as an interpreter, Magarotto told Mussolini that it was not right for the head of Italy's national association of the deaf to be a hearing person. Worse, Magarotto said, the law required it. A deaf person could not apply for the job! Mussolini must change the law.

According to Caesare Magarotto, his father talked to Mussolini like he talked to everyone else. This is not easy in Italian because in Italian there are two different words for "you." When talking to friends, children, and animals Italians say "tu", when talking with strangers and superiors, they must be polite and say "voi."

But for Magarotto's father, the world had neither strangers nor superiors. The world had only equals and friends. "It was 'tu' for everyone," remembered Caesare, even when he talked to Mussolini.

Shawn Richardson

Using his son for an interpreter, Magarotto approached Mussolini.

Everyone was shocked to see a deaf man talk that way to Mussolini. But Mussolini did not laugh. He agreed with Magarotto! In 1940, deaf people received the right to head their own national association— partly because of Mussolini and partly because of Magarotto. Magarotto became head of the new organization.

But Antonio Magarotto didn't stop there. He believed that deaf people needed their

Magarotto welcomed people into his home for a worldwide meeting of deaf people. Today's insignia for the World Federation of the Deaf is in the background.

own international organization, too. In 1951, Caesare helped his father print invitations to a worldwide meeting of deaf people. Mostly European deaf people came, crowding into the Magarotto home. At the meeting, the World Federation of the Deaf was born. Today the World Federation of the Deaf is affiliated with the United Nations. Many countries are members—and all countries must have majority deaf representation.

Antonio grew up in Rome, Italy. He lost his hearing when he was three years old. Determined to learn Italian, he read all of the time, writing down and memorizing long lists of vocabulary. Antonio had one goal for his life, Caesare said: Helping other deaf people. "My father's life was a great sacrifice," said Caesare Magarotto. "But it was for a great cause."

Gallaudet University Archives

Harriet Martineau
1802-1876

She reached out to the world with her pen.

The Writer Who Opened Minds

IN 1821, THOMAS Martineau picked up the newspaper in his home in Norwich, England. He began to read and became very excited. "There is a new writer in this newspaper," he told everyone around him, "and he writes very well."

Harriet Martineau, his sister, was very quiet. She knew who the writer was, but she was too nervous to tell her brother. Thomas continued to praise the new author. Harriet continued to say nothing. Suddenly Thomas turned to his sister in frustration. Why was she so quiet he demanded? Did she not enjoy the new writer? Why should she be so stingy about praising him?

Finally Harriet told her brother the truth. She had been too embarrassed to admit it, she said, but she herself had written the article in the newspaper. She herself was the writer. She had written under a man's name.

Thomas was shocked. He always knew his sister was a little different from most English women. But this! Writing for a newspaper? Without even asking for permission! Minutes passed before Thomas could congratulate his sister.

Harriet Martineau understood her brother's surprise and hesitation. She knew that women didn't usually write for newspapers. Harriet, an unmarried woman whose father was dead, should have turned to Thomas, her brother, for advice about writing.

But Harriet Martineau had not asked for anyone's advice. She had written an article and sent it to the newspaper on her own. She was independent, stubborn, ambitious—and a very good writer.

What is Women's Work

Harriet Martineau had been impatient with what people called "women's work" all her life. Ever since she was a little girl, she had made bonnets, knitted stockings, and covered shoes with silk cloth, like other English ladies. She had done household chores; she had cleaned, cooked, and always helped her mother.

But she made time to read, too. Every morning, she got up early to study Latin. She would study until the sun came up. Then she would go work on her household chores.

Her mother complained often about Harriet. She felt that her daughter was not behaving as a proper English lady. Her mother also complained because she felt Harriet wasn't pretty. Harriet was too thin, too pale, and often sick.

Deafness Opens

"There's a new writer in this newspaper," her brother said.

When Harriett was a little girl, she was hard-of-hearing. At 14 years old, she became completely deaf. At first Harriet told her family that she could not hear well, but they did not believe her. They accused her of faking. Then they realized that Harriet really could not hear, became angry, and accused her of not being honest about her deafness!

Years later, Harriet wrote about her first year as a deaf girl. She felt "deafness opening upon" her, she wrote, and she "vowed to be patient."

"This will kill me or cure me," she wrote in her diary. She had seen her family make fun of other deaf people and she promised herself she would never do anything to cause her family to make fun of her. She would not ask them to talk slowly. She would never ask them to change position so she could read their lips. She would not ask them to tell her what people said at parties. She would stay very quiet and she would never bother anyone.

Despite Harriet's efforts to please, her family sent her away. It was the doctor's best advice, they said. Harriet should go live with her aunt. Harriet was homesick at her aunt's house, but at least her aunt was kind to her and sent her to school. She did not return to her family until she graduated.

Harriet was 19 years old when she wrote her first story. She didn't know it, but she was on her way to becoming a famous journalist.

Money Problems

Martineau's father died in 1826, and the bank that held her family's money went bankrupt. For the first time Harriet and her sisters had to figure out how to support themselves. Some of her sisters got married, or went to live with other families and take care of their children. Martineau decided to try to earn her living in a different way; she decided to become a writer.

First she had to find people to support her by financing the publication of her first articles. Most of her relatives found a little money to give her. But some of them thought her

She became famous for her sharp pen.

Shawn Richardson

plan was silly. "I would rather give you money to earn a living with your needle," wrote one cousin. Women were supposed to sew, not write, his letter added. Martineau was insulted. She quickly returned that cousin's money.

Finally she collected enough money to publish her articles. Under the title "Illustrations of Political Economy," she tried to explain in everyday language what the words "economy" and "economics" mean. Anxiously, Martineau waited to learn if her writing would sell. It did. More copies were printed and they sold too. Martineau realized she was a success.

She began to write more. She wrote biographies, fiction, history, poetry, religious works, and children's stories. She wrote books and sent newspaper articles to the famous author and editor Charles Dickens. She translated French writings in philosophy into English. She traveled to the United States and Egypt and wrote about her travels in both countries.

Martineau wrote for a purpose. She wanted to make the world a better place. She wrote against forcing children to work in factories. She wrote against rich people taking advantage of poor people. She became famous for her sharp pen and independent thought. In a religious age, she criticized some Christian beliefs. To the horror of some of her readers, she compared Moses to Plato, and Christianity to Islam.

When she came to America, Martineau found a new horror to write about. In America, slavery was still legal and some people owned slaves. Out of curiosity, Martineau visited a meeting of Abolitionists, people who wanted to free the slaves.

She did not plan to speak there, but the Abolitionist leaders heard that a famous English writer was in the audience, and asked her to give a talk. Martineau could not refuse. She gave her anti-slavery opinion in the strongest words she could find.

When some Americans learned of Martineau's anti-slavery feelings, they were furious. Some rich people stopped inviting her to their parties. Some politicians refused to let her interview them. Worse, letter writers threatened to kill her. One writer said he would hang her; another writer said he would cut out her tongue. Martineau had planned to travel south, but after all the hateful letters, she canceled her trip.

When she died in 1876, Martineau had written 30 books and thousands of articles. She was 74 years old.

Pierre de Ronsard
1524-1585

When hearing loss forced Ronsard to leave the French court, he turned to writing poetry—and changed the writing of a civilization.

Noble Poet

IT WAS 1536 when the King of France called Pierre de Ronsard to service in his court. Ronsard was not surprised—even though he was only 12 years old. Wealthy and noble, Ronsard and his family were always ready to leave their large home in the French countryside and serve their king and their country.

Ronsard's father was in the king's court when his young son arrived there. Ronsard became a page for the son of the king. As a page, Ronsard would serve the prince and perhaps learn how to become a soldier.

The prince died young, and Pierre became a page for his brother. But the brother gave Ronsard to his sister, Princess Madeline. Ronsard was her wedding present! By this time, Ronsard was well-trained. He had learned how to walk gracefully. He had learned to use good manners at the table, chewing with his mouth half open, and his hands politely placed on the table. He had learned the proper way to treat ladies. Most importantly, he was good in sports. He used a sword well and he was learning to use other weapons of war.

When spring came, Princess Madeline married James V, the handsome and fun-loving King of Scotland. All of France rejoiced at the wedding. Then the new Queen Madeline, her husband, King James, her doctor, her ladies in waiting, her cook, her musicians, Ronsard, and eight other pages packed their bags. They were off to their new home in Scotland.

As soon as she arrived in Scotland, Queen Madeline fell sick. The country had planned to celebrate, but now no one celebrated. Everyone waited for Queen Madeline to get well. She never did. Every day, she got sicker. Within the year, she was dead, leaving behind a sad husband and all of the people she had brought with her from France.

Ronsard and the rest of the French people waited in Scotland for their country to call them home. Without his queen to serve, Ronsard had a lot of free time. He used it to take long walks in the Scottish countryside. Later, he would say that he began to write poetry there. He did not take his writing seriously, of course; no one took poetry seriously in those days. Poetry, like riding horses, was an amusement for noble people—nothing more.

After a year, Ronsard boarded a ship to return to France. The seas were rough and the boat he was in almost sank. But he arrived safely in France. Only 15 years old, he had seen many people die around him, and he almost died himself. Luckily, his own future looked bright.

In Paris, Ronsard entered the Royal Riding School. He was handsome, strong, and quick to learn new things. When Lazare de Baif, one of the highest men in the royal court, needed a group of people to go to Germany, he picked Ronsard.

Becoming Deaf

In Germany, Ronsard's life changed, but not the way he had hoped. He became very sick and ran a high fever. When he recovered, he could not hear people talk. He had to watch their lips carefully to understand what they said. He was "demi-sourd," people said, "half-deaf."

His dreams of being a soldier or a diplomat ended. He returned home and turned again to writing poetry. He wrote mostly in Latin, the language of educated noblemen and the great books of ancient Rome. He wrote a few French poems, too, just for fun.

In 1542, his father came home to visit his deaf son. Ronsard, now 18,

Walking through lush countryside, Ronsard composed his first poems.

had been home for two years. His father wanted him to get a job. "You could study law," the older man suggested. But Ronsard shook his head; he hated law. Ronsard's father could think of only one other way for his son to earn money: Ronsard would become a priest.

Ronsard and his father traveled to the town of LeMans, where Ronsard took vows to become a priest. While he was there, Ronsard got up his courage and showed his poetry to Jacques Peletier du Man. Peletier du Man was an expert in geometry, medicine, Greek, and Latin, and one of the most famous thinkers in France. When Peletier du Man finished reading the poems, he gave the young poet some advice: "Write in French," he urged. "French is as good as any ancient language."

Becoming a Poet

Perhaps Ronsard was amazed by du Man's words. In truth, he had probably felt frustrated writing in Latin. He respected Latin and he knew it well. He had studied its grammar; he had memorized its rules. But Ronsard's favorite language was French, the language that he and his friends used every day. Now here was Peletier du Man, the most respected thinker in his whole country, urging him to write in his own language, the language that he really preferred.

With his hair cut short like a priest, Ronsard returned to the Royal Riding School. But he was no longer satisfied there. He wanted to focus on his writing.

Sometimes Ronsard would leave the riding school, sneaking off to visit Lazare de Baif, the same man with whom he had gone to Germany. Ronsard, Baif, and Baif's 11-year-old son talked about poetry, Greece, Rome, language, and the new feeling in the air of France. Some people called the new feeling *humanism*. The humanists loved the literature of ancient Rome and Greece, and they wanted to write about their own country, their own time—and in their own language.

When his father died, Ronsard stopped pretending to be a priest-soldier for the king. He entered a new school, the Collège de Coqueret, and became a full-time student. At the Collège de Coqueret, he studied Greek and Latin and the writings of ancient authors. He wrote too—almost always in French. He wrote poems about nature, France, beauty, pleasure, life, love, and death. He began a grand poem about the history of France.

Shawn Richardson

Ronsard converses with his friends.

While he was a student, he became friends with Joachim Du Bellay, who was also deaf. While Ronsard usually preferred speech and lipreading to communicate, Du Bellay usually communicated by writing.

Du Bellay, Ronsard, and the other French students formed a group like a club, called "La Pléiade," after a constellation of stars named for Greek goddesses. Ronsard was called the "Prince of Poets," the "Chief" of La Pléiade, and the most celebrated poet in Europe.

In 1550, Ronsard published *Odes*, his first book of poetry. It was a great success. In 1552, he published *Loves*, a book of poems about a young girl with whom he had fallen in love. The French people loved Ronsard's books of poetry. For 20 years, Ronsard wrote and published poetry. Even as he was dying, he wrote poetry, working on his will in between his poems.

When he died in 1585, no one doubted that the language of France was as great as the language of ancient Rome, or that French writers were as great as the great Latin writers. Ronsard's poems helped to establish French as a language of great power and beauty.

Gallaudet University Archives

Laura Catherine Redden Searing
1840-1923

*With her ever-present slate and pen, she covered
the Civil War and wrote for a reborn nation.*

Journalist for America

IN ST. LOUIS, Missouri in 1856, people fought in the streets as the United States drifted toward Civil War. Missouri was a slave state, even though many Missourians were against slavery. The anti-slavery Missourians wanted to join the Union and fight for freedom. New pro-Union articles began to appear in the newspapers. Some people cheered for the articles and others tore them up.

The author of the controversial articles was Howard Glyndon. The people demanded to know who Howard Glyndon was. The people who supported the Union praised him; people who supported slavery wanted to hang him.

When people learned that "Howard Glyndon" was a teenage girl, they were shocked. "Howard's" real name was Laura Redden, and she was still in school, completing her senior year at the Missouri School for the Deaf. Supporters of the Union were embarrassed, and enemies of the Union laughed.

But Laura Redden was undaunted. When she came home, she continued to work for the newspaper. She began to write poetry too. Soon she would become one of the best-loved writers in America.

Deaf at 11

Laura Redden was born hearing. Her family was known for its writing and poetry. Her great-grandfather had been a poet in England.

Laura became deaf when she was 11 years old. One day, she came home from school feeling sick and tired. She didn't eat. She didn't talk to anyone. She lay down on her bed, fully clothed, and stayed there for weeks.

When she began to get well again, she saw her mother and the doctor talking. She knew that they were talking because they were looking at each other, making faces, and moving their mouths. Laura watched carefully. Before when people moved their mouths like that, she had heard their voices. Now she heard nothing.

She called to her mother and the doctor. Slowly everyone realized that she had lost her hearing. Nothing hurt, she wrote later in a newspaper article about her deafness. She was just deaf. She grew well and strong again.

The only thing that changed was her voice and it changed almost immediately. Laura knew her voice was different because she saw people's faces when she tried to talk. Instead of listening to her words, they only listened to her tone.

"You don't talk right," her family told her. "Better stop. Better not use your voice at all."

At first, Laura felt hurt. When she was hearing, she had a good voice. She had loved to sing and to tell stories. Reluctantly, she paid attention to the advice of her family and the faces of her friends. She rarely used her voice.

Her family sent her to the Missouri School for the Deaf (MSD). At school, Laura learned sign language and fingerspelling. Finally Laura could talk with people again. Of course, she couldn't use speech. Instead she used signs. With people who did not know sign language, she used her slate and pencil.

She graduated from MSD in two years. When she returned home, she wrote full-time for the *St. Louis Republican*, the newspaper that supported the Union and Abraham Lincoln, the Republican candidate for President of the United States.

When President Lincoln was elected and war broke out between the North and the South, some Missourians rebelled. They wanted to join the Confederacy. Laura, still a strong supporter of the Union and President Lincoln, and still using the name of Howard Glyndon, wrote a poem. She called it "Belle Missouri." Here is part of her poem:

> *The precious blood of all thy slain*
> *Arises from each reeking plain.*
> *Wipe out this foul disloyal stain.*
> *Belle Missouri! My Missouri!*

Missouri's Union soldiers loved the poem. They made it their song and sang it throughout the Civil War.

When the *St. Louis Republican* needed a reporter in Washington, D.C., the editors picked Laura Redden, now a young woman. Laura had been born in Maryland, near Washington, D.C., so perhaps she felt she was returning home. In Washington, D.C., Laura Redden impressed everyone. Her stories and poetry became famous not only in Washington and Missouri, but throughout the United States.

General Ulysses S. Grant invited her to travel with him to the battlefield. It was rare for a woman to be invited to the battlefield. It was dangerous, too, but Redden didn't care. She was glad to accept the invitation. She wrote poems about the Union soldiers and Generals Grant and Mitchell. She wrote about the lives of congressmen, calling her book *Notable Men of the House of Representatives.*

As the war continued, she became as impressed with its tragedy as with its glory. For example, in the poem "Bringing Him Home," she wrote of the death of a soldier.

Here is part of the poem:

Why mother! What's the matter?
How you stare! Why won't you
let me see the letter, too?
Why do you hide it?

When she finished her book of war poetry, she gave it to President Lincoln. President Lincoln read the poems and enjoyed them. "They are all patriotic," wrote Lincoln, "and some very pretty."

Redden also wrote about her deafness. She called the poem "My Story." In 1865 as the war ended, Redden sailed for Europe. In Europe, she learned that President Lincoln had been shot. Saddened, she wrote a poem about him.

In Europe, she visited with the nobility and writers of many countries. She learned French, German, and Italian, and sent her stories back to America's top newspapers and magazines. She also did some work for the U.S. government, collecting information about silkworm production for the Department of Agriculture.

When she returned to the United States, she published her book of poetry, *Sounds from Secret Chambers*. She also learned about the Clarke School, a new school for deaf students in Northampton, Massachusetts, which taught speech and lipreading.

Shawn Richardson

Patrolling the front lines with General Grant.

Perhaps the teachers at Clarke School wondered why a woman so successful with her writing would show up on their doorstep, but there she was. Laura Redden was determined to learn to use her voice to speak again.

She spent hours, days, and weeks practicing with her teachers. They were ready to give up, she said, but she refused. She kept trying to make the sounds that would correspond to the sound of her old voice.

Finally she did it. Her teacher couldn't believe it, she wrote. The teacher thought that another student had made the sound. When the teacher learned it was Redden, the whole school rejoiced, she said.

Now she had the right sound, but still the words came out wrong. By coincidence, a famous teacher visited her school at about this time—Alexander Graham Bell. Her teachers, perhaps impressed with the determination of their student, took her problem to him.

Bell was from Scotland and full of enthusiasm for teaching deaf people. His mother was deaf and he himself married a deaf woman. Even after he invented the telephone, he would tell people that the part of his life that he enjoyed most was teaching deaf students.

Bell watched and listened as Redden tried to talk. Finally he diagnosed her speech problem. Most people talk only when they breathe out, but Redden was trying to talk while she breathed in, too. Then she would get out of breath and her voice would sound strange. Redden practiced her new way of speaking with her friends and felt satisfied.

Her next task was learning to lipread. She went to another new school in Mystic, Connecticut. She worked hard at the new school, too, but the woman who wrote English beautifully and mastered many languages, never understood speech on the lips. She struggled and struggled. Finally she decided she had no time for such a skill. She would stick with her pencil and slate!

In 1876 at 36 years old, Redden married a rich and successful New York lawyer. His name was Edward Searing. Redden became Laura Redden Searing. Soon afterward, she bore a child, a little girl.

As she grew older, she continued to write poetry. She became friends with many famous American poets, and exchanged letters with them. She also became involved with the Convention of American Instructors of the Deaf (CAID), a newly formed organization of teachers of deaf students.

Her daughter grew up, married, and moved to California. Soon afterward, CAID had a national meeting there. Redden and her husband packed up their bags and went to California and never returned to New York. She loved California. Her poem, "The Hills of Santa Cruz," about the land near her home, became famous.

Later her daughter moved to Fairbanks, Alaska. Redden, now an older woman, followed her there. In Fairbanks, she wrote "The First Dog Team Over the Rail," a poem that won a prize and became famous throughout the state.

Although she believed in speech, Redden Searing always believed in sign language too. In her poem to her beloved President Lincoln, she wrote that when God called Lincoln to heaven, he used a sign.

She died in 1923 at 83 years old.

Erastus "Deaf" Smith
1787-1837

Today Texas is part of the United States,
thanks in part to this scout and spy.

Deaf Scout Leads Fight for Freedom

FROM THE MOMENT he entered the dry, craggy land in the early 1800s, Erastus Smith loved Texas and decided to make his home there. Some of Smith's American neighbors were angry that Texas belonged to Mexico. But Smith didn't care. He learned Spanish, married a Mexican woman, and became a Mexican citizen.

Although they didn't always get along with each other, most of the Americans and Mexicans respected Smith. He was a brave fighter. He could hunt buffalo as well as the Indians, and he was one of the best scouts and marksmen in the land.

Smith was quiet and serious. When people talked in groups, he would stand at a distance, look away, and wait until they finished. He preferred to talk with people on a one-to-one basis, probably because he had to lipread them. Smith had been deaf since he was a baby. The Mexicans called him "El Sordo"; the Americans called him "Deaf Smith."

Like many of his American neighbors, Smith was not born in Texas. He came from the wooded countryside of New York State. When he was 11 years old, his parents moved to Mississippi. They bought land there and raised Smith and his brothers and sisters. When he was 23 years old, Smith headed west by himself. He traveled through Missouri and made his way into Texas. He settled in San Antonio, a tiny town in the heart of the wild land north of the Rio Grande. Smith tried to ignore the bad feelings between his Mexican and American neighbors. All he wanted to do was shoot buffalo, guide hunters, trade with his neighbors, raise a few animals, and take care of his family.

Men at War

When fighting broke out between the Americans and Mexicans in 1835, Smith tried to ignore it. At first that was difficult; then it was impossible.

One day Smith returned from hunting buffalo to find angry Americans surrounding San Antonio. At first, the Americans would not allow Smith through to see his family.

Smith went to the leader of the Americans, General Stephen Austin, to ask him for permission to ride through the American fighters. Austin knew Smith well and he tried to persuade him to join his army. Smith refused. He just wanted to go home, where his wife waited with their children.

Austin finally gave permission and Smith rode through the line of American fighters. Inside San Antonio, Mexican soldiers were ready for battle. Smith asked the Mexicans for permission to enter the town. The Mexican general was General Coz, the brother-in-law of Santa Anna, Dictator of Mexico and Commander of the Mexican army.

Coz asked Smith to ride out and discuss the matter with him, so

Smith realized the soldiers were shooting at him.

Smith rode out to talk with the Mexican general. As they talked, Smith noticed a group of Mexican soldiers racing toward him on horseback.

Suspecting a trick, he turned to escape. Suddenly furious, General Coz swung at Smith with his sword and slashed his head. Blood streamed through Smith's hair and down his face, but he ignored it, racing his horse back toward the Americans. The Mexican soldiers chased him and Smith noticed flecks of earth spit up from the ground near his own galloping horse. He realized that the Mexicans were shooting at him.

The American fighters saw what was happening and sped out to meet him, their guns blazing at the Mexicans. Outnumbered, the Mexicans retreated to their own camp.

Smith was outraged. Within hours he found General Austin and told him that he wanted to fight for the Americans. Austin was thrilled. He immediately made Smith an officer. One of Smith's first acts as a Texas army officer was to get his family safely out of San Antonio. He took them to an American army camp, where they would be safe until the war ended.

A Price for His Head!

Furious at Smith's escape, General Coz offered $1,000 to anyone who could prove that they killed him. Smith was not amused. He put a price on General Coz's head too—but only $500. "That's all his head is worth," he told people.

In 1835, Smith led a group of Texans under Jim Bowie, the legendary American frontiersman, in a sneak attack against the Mexican soldiers. Smith fired the first shot of the battle which later became known as the Battle of Concepcion.

After that, General Houston put Smith in charge of a company of fighters. With his frontier skills and knowledge of the countryside, Smith became Houston's top scout and spy. No one in Texas dared to call Smith by his first name, "Erastus," and Houston wouldn't either. Instead he began to call him "The Wonderful Mr. E.," a name that stuck throughout the war.

Smith became famous for his bravery in battle. It is said that once General Houston saw that his men were losing a battle and yelled for them to retreat. Though Smith couldn't hear his general's order, he must have seen the soldiers retreating around him. Nevertheless he kept fighting. Perhaps embarrassed to see Smith fighting alone, the hearing men returned to the battlefield.

Alamo Scout

Smith was visiting his family when General Santa Anna, Mexico's dictator, led his whole army into Texas. The Mexicans went to San Antonio, where they forced the Americans to retreat into a small mission called the Alamo. There were 187 American fighters in the Alamo, and they were surrounded by Santa Anna and 5000 professional soldiers. The Americans refused to surrender and Santa Anna attacked. The Americans fought hard. Even after their ammunition ran out, they continued to resist. Most of them died fighting, using their fists and rifle butts against the triumphant Mexicans.

When Sam Houston learned about the fight at the Alamo, he sent Smith to get more information about the battle. On the way, Smith met a woman travelling with two servants and a baby. She was the wife of an Alamo officer. It was true, she told Smith. The Mexicans had captured the Alamo. All of the Alamo fighters were dead. Santa Anna killed his prisoners because he wanted to teach the rebellious Americans a lesson. For Texas fighting men, capture meant death.

"Remember the Alamo!" cried the Americans after that. It was a bold and determined cry. But no one really thought that the Americans would win the war. The Mexicans had professional soldiers. The Americans were farmers, hunters, and family men, who believed they were fighting for their freedom. Furthermore, the Mexicans outnumbered the Americans, almost 30-1.

As a result, most of the time, the Americans avoided battle. Many of the men complained that Houston knew only how to retreat, but Sam Houston knew better than to fight the huge Mexican army at one time. Instead, the American army used guerrilla tactics, shooting at the Mexican army and running away, instead of trying to fight a pitched battle.

As his chief scout, Smith helped Houston learn about the Mexican troop movements. Once, he captured the man who was carrying Santa Anna's personal mail. The Americans laughed when Smith turned up dressed in the mail carrier's uniform. He put on the man's sombrero and his Mexican army pants that didn't quite reach his ankles. Next to him was the hapless mail carrier, standing in Smith's dirty frontier clothes, and looking very unhappy.

Another time, Smith and another scout tracked the Mexicans back to their camp. While the other scout watched, Smith took off his army boots, rolled up his pants, and pulled his shirt loose around his pants. Then he pushed a large sombrero down over his red hair and wandered absent-mindedly into the enemy camp.

The Mexicans ignored him—just as Smith had thought they would. He walked about the camp slowly, trying to learn what he could with his eyes. When people spoke to him, he mumbled a reply in Spanish and kept walking. Finally Smith finished his work and the two men galloped back to the American camp, where Smith told Houston everything that he had seen.

American Victory

Some historians credit the American victory battle to Smith. Sam Houston and his men followed the Mexican army to the San Jacinto River, secretly camped nearby, and planned a surprise attack. Some of Smith's men noticed that if the bridge across the river were cut down, the Mexicans would be trapped. Smith liked the idea and took it to Houston.

"Can you do it?" Houston asked his scout. "Can you cut down the bridge?"

"Give me six men," said Smith. "I will try."

Houston nodded. Smith got his six men. Together, they sneaked passed the enemy, and destroyed the bridge.

The next day, the Americans readied their attack. They knew that it was a Mexican custom to eat a big meal at noon and take a siesta afterwards. They launched their surprise attack during the siesta. Waking up from their sleep, the Mexican leaders tried to escape across the bridge, only to find that Smith and his men had destroyed it.

The Mexican soldiers were trapped. In less than an hour, the Americans killed or captured all of them. It was a great victory. The Americans, numbering 780 men, had killed 600 soldiers and captured 600 soldiers, and only two Americans had died in the fighting.

Smith would tell Houston everything he saw.

Shawn Richardson

117

Courtesy of the state of Texas

Sam Houston accepts the surrender of the Mexicans, with his trusted deaf scout, the "Wonderful Mr. E.," at his side.

Smith captured the beautiful black horse that belonged to General Santa Anna during the battle. He gave it to General Houston, who later sold it back to Santa Anna, giving money from the sale to the young government of Texas. Santa Anna himself was captured the next day.

General Coz, the general who had wounded Smith at the beginning of the war, was captured, too. Smith may have wanted to kill Coz, but now he couldn't. As an American, Smith could not kill any prisoner or any Mexican soldier who surrendered.

In defeat, Santa Anna signed the treaty that made Texas independent. A famous painting shows Santa Anna surrendering to Sam Houston, with his trusted scout, "The Wonderful Mr. E.," his hand cupped behind one of his deaf ears, at Houston's side.

Smith returned home, an honored hero of the revolution. The Texas government granted him 2,655 acres of land, enough for a huge home and farm. In addition, when the new nation of Texas printed money, the government put the face of Deaf Smith on its five-dollar bills.

Unfortunately Smith did not live long to enjoy his honors. He died less than two years later. It is said that no member of his family came to his funeral and that he was buried in an unmarked grave. He was fifty years old.

Although Deaf Smith's face went out of circulation with Texas five-dollar bills, today his name is still famous. "Deaf Smith Peanut Butter" and "Deaf Smith County Wheat" are enjoyed by people everywhere—some of them in Deaf Smith County, Texas.

Denki Tani Sanzan

Sanzan Tani
1802-1867

This deaf and blind scholar became
one of the greatest teachers in Japan.

Scholar by Touch

IN THE MID-1800s, a young Japanese student carefully practiced writing invisible letters with his forefinger in the palm of his hand. He was on his way to meet a famous teacher, Sanzan Tani, one of the most learned men in Japan. Tani was deaf and blind and communicated with his students through touch.

Tani had become deaf when he was eight years old. He read a lot, and his father spent most of his money on books for his son. But young Tani never felt satisfied with his reading. He had so many questions! Reading only led to more questions.

When he grew up, Tani left his village home to look for a teacher to help him understand his questions about the great books. He traveled from town to town and questioned teacher after teacher. But his curiosity was never satisfied. Surprisingly, the teachers began to tell him that he knew more about the great books than they did. Even in Kyoto, the center of Japanese culture and learning, Tani seemed to know more about the great books than anyone else.

As a child, Sanzan Tani loved to read and write.

Denki Tani Sanzan

Tani immortalized in a Japanese woodcut.

The government learned about Tani's brilliance and awarded him a teaching position. Tani taught for many years. As he taught, he lost his hearing and eyesight. He became deaf and blind.

Blind and deaf, Tani continued to teach. Students wrote their questions in the palm of his hand. Tani answered from memory. His mind was so powerful that he could tell the students where to read about their questions in the great books. He had the books filed away, page by page, in his memory.

Douglas Tilden
1860-1935

Today his sculptures adorn
the beautiful city of San Francisco.

Sculptor to the City

IN 1888, TWO young deaf Americans walked into a gallery in Paris. Douglas Tilden had never seen so many paintings and statues. He walked through the gallery in awe, looking at the work of some of France's best artists.

The painting was the best he had ever seen, he confided to his friend. But he felt differently about the sculpture. "I can do better," he signed.

A year later, Tilden finished his first sculpture in France. He sent the sculpture—a man ready to throw a baseball—to the judges for the American exhibition at the World's Fair being held in Paris. Tilden knew that the American judges would look at many American statues and pick the best ones.

He was very hopeful that they would include his statue. The American judges were not supposed to be as fussy as the French and European judges. Further, Tilden hoped that the judges would remember that baseball was a favorite American game and select his statue, *The Baseball Player*, for patriotic reasons.

Tilden presented the statue to the judges himself. When he told the judges that he was deaf, they frowned at him and fell silent. "You'll get a letter," they told him finally.

When it came, the letter was a rejection.

Surely Tilden was disappointed, but he did not give up. He asked the judges of the French exhibition area to consider his work, too. French judges were supposed to have higher standards than the American judges and Tilden waited for their decision anxiously. Finally the letter arrived. It was one word: "Accepté."

Out of the West

Douglas Tilden was born in Chico, California. His father was a doctor and his mother had crossed the continent in a wagon train. He was born on May 1st—the same day that the new California School for the Deaf opened.

From the time he was a little boy, Tilden loved to draw. His love of art may have intensified after he lost his hearing from scarlet fever when he was five years old. After that, Tilden talked to hearing people with gestures, paper, and pen. With deaf people he used sign language.

At the California School for the Deaf (CSD), Tilden was an outstanding student. His only problem was his temper. He became angry easily. Dr. Warring Wilkinson, CSD superintendent, said that once he saw Douglas walk up to another little boy and knock off his hat. Douglas was only six years old and Wilkinson walked up to him and told him firmly to pick up the hat and give it back to the other boy, but Douglas refused.

So Wilkinson led Douglas off to his office. In the privacy of his office, Wilkinson tried to scold the young boy, Douglas was unrepentant. He hit Wilkinson across the face with a long tin pillbox. Startled, Wilkinson shook him. Finally, a chastened Douglas went out, apologized to the other child, gave him a hug, and picked up his hat.

Nevertheless, Tilden became a successful student at CSD. He made the honor roll and joined the CSD debate team. He also discovered his love of art. When he was nine or ten years old, he stole some bluewash, ground it into powder, mixed it with water, and made his own paint. He still needed a paintbrush—so he nipped off a bit of his own hair and fastened it to a stick.

After he graduated from CSD, he applied to the University of California. The university accepted him, but he decided not to go there. Instead he wanted to be a mechanic, and his mother wrote superintendent Wilkinson a long letter asking the superintendent to find a job as a mechanic for her son.

Apologetically, Wilkinson wrote back, saying he was unable to find any positions because Tilden was deaf. Instead he asked Tilden to come and work at CSD. Tilden accepted. He would live and work at CSD for eight years.

Born to Sculpt

When he went home on a visit, Tilden saw that his brother had taken up sculpting. Fascinated, he asked to meet his brother's teacher. The minute he entered the teacher's sculpting studio, Tilden fell in love with the craft. ". . . What a wonderful world of new sensation," he wrote later. "It seemed to suffocate and intoxicate me . . . plaster casts of masterpieces, dead men's faces, busts, masses of white stone awaiting cutting . . . the smell of dampness, unswept floor, marble dust, delightful confusion."

He asked his brother's teacher to teach him, too, and he moved a barrel of clay into an empty building at CSD and set up his studio. From then on, he sculpted in his spare time. He enjoyed teaching, but he felt sculpting was his real work.

To learn about sculpting, Tilden knew that he would have to leave CSD. He would have to go to New York or Paris, where the world's most skilled sculptors would share the secrets of their craft.

Young Traveler

With money borrowed from CSD, Tilden traveled across the country. When he arrived in New York City, he found an apartment and a deaf roommate. He also visited one of New

York's new oral schools for deaf students. Oralism, a philosophy of teaching deaf students with speech and lipreading instead of sign language, was sweeping the world, and Tilden was curious to see how it worked. To his surprise, he arrived at the school to find teachers and students using lots of signs.

After a year, Tilden and his roommate decided to go to France. They boarded a boat and headed across the ocean. Once they arrived in Paris, they were thrilled to find a school for deaf students. In fact, the Paris school was the oldest national school for the deaf in the world.

Many deaf people lived around it, and Tilden quickly became part of the Parisian deaf community. He gave talks at the school and often visited the nearby deaf club. When the first International Congress of the World Federation of the Deaf (WFD) was held in Paris, Tilden attended and was elected vice president.

Tilden works on The Bear Hunt, *which still stands outside the California School for the Deaf in Fremont.*

At the International Congress, Tilden learned that many European schools for deaf students were becoming oral schools. Tilden hated oralism. He introduced a measure to fight it at the WFD conference. He wanted the American way of teaching—using sign language as well as speech and lipreading—to be used to teach deaf children.

The topic was hotly debated. Perhaps Tilden depended on the debate skills he had learned at CSD, because the delegates finally agreed to pass his measure. "Sign language is our language," he always said.

In Paris, Tilden met Paul Choppin, one of the best-known sculptors in Paris. Like Tilden, Choppin was deaf. He had graduated from the school for the deaf in Paris and become famous for winning sculpting contests. Even today Choppin's statues brighten the streets of Paris like Tilden's statues brighten the streets of San Francisco.

Choppin became Tilden's teacher, checking on him weekly and helping him with his work. In addition to *The Baseball Player*, Tilden made a statue entitled *The Tired Boxer*, of a well-muscled boxer, sitting down probably after an intense match. When he exhibited it in competition, *The Tired Boxer* won a bronze medal.

He also made a statue of an Indian fighting a bear. Called *The Bear Hunt*, the statue shows an Indian with his tomahawk raised against a bear whose teeth enclose his arm. Tilden wrote that he sculpted it so the winner of the battle "must forever be a question in the spectator's mind."

Tilden loved Paris. He stayed for six years. Then his money ran out and he was forced to come home.

His work arrived before he did. His sculpture, *The Baseball Player*, was exhibited in San Francisco. The other works in the exhibition were by famous foreign artists—Monet, Rembrandt, and Delacroix. Tilden was the only American artist whose work was selected.

The Return

When he returned home, Tilden was already famous as the first native artist from California who had been recognized in Europe. San Francisco was growing quickly and James Duval Phelan, a wealthy man who loved politics and art, wanted Tilden to sculpt statues that would bring beauty to the city.

With Phelan's support, Tilden sculpted. In 1897, Phelan, now newly elected mayor, unveiled Tilden's *Admission Day*, a statue of an angel who holds a book, open and empty for all to see. Tilden's implication: The history of California was still to be written in the book.

The newspapers pronounced the work excellent. Adored by politicians and the public, Tilden began work on other statues. *The Tired Boxer*, which Tilden had sculpted in Paris, found a home near the Olympic club. *The Baseball Player*, his sculpture on baseball, found a home overlooking the Golden Gate Bridge. *The Bear Hunt* ended up at the California School for the Deaf. CSD kept it because Tilden was never able to pay back the money he had borrowed from the school to continue his education. It stands there to this day.

One man who saw Tilden's work asked him to make a statue in honor of his father, a successful businessman. Tilden worked on it for months. Called *Mechanics*, the sculpture shows men hard at work. It is considered one of Tilden's best pieces.

In 1899, Tilden was appointed professor at the Mark Hopkins Art Institute, part of the University of California. Tilden was relaxed about teaching hearing college students. When someone asked him how he would communicate with them, he smiled: "I could talk to them in three languages (French, English, or American Sign Language)," he said. "But I mean to make them work."

He used a combination of pencil and gesture to get his point across. In France, it was normal for art students to paint and make sculptures of models who wore no clothing. Perhaps because of his experience there, Tilden became the first teacher in California to introduce nude modeling in the university classroom.

University of California Library

The Tired Boxer, *sculpted by Tilden in Paris, was destroyed in the California earthquake of 1906.*

Even at his busiest, Tilden continued working with and for deaf people. He helped to organize the California Association of the Deaf and drafted its constitution and bylaws. In 1909, he was elected its president.

In 1895, Tilden married one of his former students at CSD. He had known her before he left for Europe. When he came back, their friendship turned to love.

While Tilden was in Oregon finishing up a bronze statue, the earthquake of 1906 destroyed San Francisco and left 700 people dead. His beloved *Tired Boxer* was in pieces, but his other statues remained standing, the debris of the city scattered at their feet.

He wrote his friend and political leader Phelan that he wanted to return home immediately with a statue titled *California Volunteers*. Sculpted to commemorate the men who had served in the Spanish-American War, the statue seemed to show California's determination to recover from the devastating earthquake. Phelan quickly agreed to his plan, and the unveiling of *California Volunteers* was Tilden's last great triumph.

California and the rest of the nation began to suffer hard economic times. Businesses made less money and no one was able to pay Tilden for his large statues. Tilden suffered hard times, too. He had marriage problems and finally got a divorce. He asked CSD, his old school, to let him come back and teach, but CSD refused.

Finally he asked his friend Phelan to help him get a job as a mechanic. Phelan did. Tilden laughed about getting a job as an old man that he had wanted in his youth. He worked as a mechanic during the day and continued to sculpt in his spare time. In 1935, a friend found him dead in his studio. He had apparently died while working. He was 75 years old.

Konstantin Tsiolkovsky
1857-1935

*Before the first airplane, this Russian scientist was working
on plans to launch the world into the Space Age.*

Seeing the Space Age

IN 1957, A ROCKET blasted through the earth's atmosphere and a satellite slid into orbit. People stood back in awe. It was the first time human beings had thrust anything high enough into the atmosphere to orbit the earth. Until then no one had been sure it was even possible.

The Space Age had dawned.

In America, people were not only surprised, they were also a little nervous and scared. Why? The satellite did not belong to them. The people who considered themselves the leaders of the free world had not yet succeeded in making and launching satellites. Instead, the Russians had done it. The satellite, Sputnik I, was Russian. The Russians were leading the world into space.

How did the Russians do it? The reason was partly Konstantin Tsiolkovsky. Deaf since he was nine years old, Tsiolkovsky had dreamed of travelling into space all his life and developed the math for the world's first spaceship and satellite. The Soviets called him the "Father of the Space Age."

River Boy

Konstantin Tsiolkovsky was born in the tiny Russian village of Izhevskoye. His family was poor. His father lost his job and spent much of his time at home, tinkering with inventions and crafts. His mother was devoted to her family, stretching every ruble to make sure her family had food and clothes.

When Tsiolkovsky grew older, his family moved to Ryazan, a town on a river. Young Tsiolkovsky loved the river, swimming in summer, shoe-skating in winter, and jumping from ice flow to ice flow, making his way to the next bank when the ice broke up in spring.

At nine years old, Tsiolkovsky became sick with scarlet fever. As he recovered, he realized he was deaf. At first, being deaf was hard for him. He was not sure how to act around the other children. He felt that they made fun of him. He felt embarrassed.

He stopped going to school and his mother taught him to read and write at home. When he was 13 years old, his mother died. Tsiolkovsky began to work on his own, studying his brother's schoolbooks. Then he passed the exam for high school. He struggled hard in high school. There were no interpreters and he could not understand the teacher.

He continued to read on his own, especially books about science. He also began trying his own experiments. Scraping together materials, he tried to make a carriage that would use steam power instead of horsepower. The idea failed, but Tsiolkovsky continued to experiment. He designed lathes and windmills. He made his own hearing aids, little metal funnels that curved out of his ears.

Shoe-skating on winter ice.

Shawn Richardson

When he left high school, his father gave him a little bit of money and sent him to Moscow to study. Perhaps Tsiolkovsky was thrilled to be in Moscow, the capital of Russia, where the tsars lived in the Kremlin and famous professors taught at the university. But perhaps he was mostly scared.

Moscow Student

He entered the big city alone, a poor country boy in search of a room. A lady who did laundry in a rich family's home agreed to rent him a room. The rent took almost all the money he had.

In Moscow, Tsiolkovsky set up a routine. Every morning he went to the public library, entering as soon as the doors opened. Inside the library, he gathered up some books, sat down, and read. When the day ended and the librarian turned off the kerosene lamp and closed the doors, Tsiolkovsky would get up slowly, put on his coat to protect himself from the Russian winter, and go home.

With almost no money, he lived on bread and water. He became thin. His hair was uncut. His clothing hung like rags. He didn't care. He lived to read, experiment, and explore ideas. In Moscow, people traveled by horse and buggy, but Tsiolkovsky was already planning space travel.

Sometimes his thoughts would make him so excited, he couldn't sleep. Then he would walk the streets of Moscow, sometimes all night long, figuring out how to make ideas work— how to drive a rocket out of the earth's orbit and into space.

With no teacher and no school, he read only what interested him. In his second year in Moscow, he taught himself calculus and spherical trigonometry.

At 22 years old, he went back home. He studied to become a teacher, passed the teacher's exam, and got a job teaching physics in a nearby high school. He married Varvara Yevgrafovna Sokolova. Like his mother, Sokolova did not care about money and believed that Tsiolkovsky's work was more important than financial success. Also like his mother, Sokolova knew how to keep her family fed and clothed with very little money. Tsiolkovsky and his family ate better when he began teaching. They could afford vegetables with their bread.

Dreams and Math

As a teacher, Tsiolkovsky had very little time for his experiments. He taught classes all day and came home at night exhausted. When school ended for a two-month winter vacation, Tsiolkovsky wrote his first article for publication. In the article, he described what life would be like for the human race in space. It was published in Russia's top scientific journal. In 1895, he wrote another article, "A Dream of Earth and Sky."

In 1903, he wrote about exploring space, focusing on how to get there. Tsiolkovsky wrote about rockets that would break apart in stages—just as rockets do today. He calculated the best angle and speed to get the rocket out of gravity and into orbit. He calculated how big rockets should be and what their shape should be. He devised a math formula—now called the Tsiolkovsky formula—to explain the motion of a rocket and its size. He also calculated the angle of blast-off.

Shawn Richardson

Studying alone in his library, Tsiolkovsky mastered calculus and trigonometry.

At the University in Moscow, the professors were pleased. In 1917, when the tsar was overthrown and the Communist Party took power in Russia, the Soviet government recognized the value of Tsiolkovsky's work immediately.

Tsiolkovsky became famous. He was elected to the prestigious Soviet Academy. As he grew older, the government gave him a pension, made him an honorary member of the Air Force Academy, and bought him a bigger house. All of his work—everything he had ever written—was published and republished. In competition with the United States and anxious to show the whole world that Communism was a superior form of government, the Soviets were grateful to Tsiolkovsky, whom they saw as the ticket to their country's success in space.

When a Russian reporter visited him in his home near the end of his life, the reporter wrote that Tsiolkovsky still talked of space travel. ". . . The two of us were living on two different floors—I on earth and Tsiolkovsky in the universe," wrote the reporter. "It seemed to me that I had met a prophet."

While most of Tsiolkovsky's dreams have come true, others remain to be explored. For example, Tsiolkovsky was very interested in energy from the sun. "We only use two billionths of it," he wrote, "and we should use more. As land on the earth becomes overused or committed to housing, perhaps we will want to take full advantage of the sun's light—and garden our vegetables in outer space."

When a nine-volume history of space exploration was printed, Tsiolkovsky's life filled one full volume. To this day, Russians honor Tsiolkovsky as the Father of the Space Age. In 1967, a crater on the moon was named after him.

In 1935, Tsiolkovsky died in old age. He was 78.

References

Some of these references may be hard to find, but if you enjoy reading biographies, it is worth the effort.

ALICE   Alexandra Queen of Yugoslavia. Prince Philip: *A Family Portrait*. Paris: Opera Mundi. 1960.

BEETHOVEN   Wendy Thompson. *The Composer's World*. New York: Viking. 1994.

CLERC   Cathryn Carroll. *Clerc: The Early Years* Washington, DC: Gallaudet University Press. 1991.

GOYA   Pierre Gassier. *Goya*. New York: Rizzoli International Publications. 1955.

Sonnenstrahl Deborah. "Francisco Goya's Art: Before & After His Deafness." July, Aug. *Voice*, pp.7-9. 1988.

HOY   "The Colorful Legend of Dummy Hoy." *Deaf Life*, Part I, November, pages 10-19 and 22-29; Part II December, 1992, p.10-19 and 22-31.

KELLER   Helen Keller. *The Story of My Life*. New York: Doubleday. 1954.

LOW   Gladys Denny Schultz and Daisy Gordon Lawrence. *Lady from Savannah*. New York: Girl Scouts USA. 1958.

SMITH   Cleburne Huston. *Deaf Smith: The Incredible Texas Spy*. Texas: Texan Press. 1973.

TILDEN   Mildred Pierce. *Douglas Tilden: Deaf Sculptor*. Maryland: T.J. Publishers. 1980.

Mildred Albronda, *Douglas Tilden: The Man and His Legacy*: California: Emerald Point Press. 1994.

DEAF CULTURE & HISTORY

These books are about language, culture, and people.

Bowe, Frank. *Changing the Rules*. Maryland: T.J. Publishers. 1986.

Christiansen, John & Barnatt, Sharon. Deaf President Now: The 1988 Revolution at Gallaudet University. Washington, DC: Gallaudet University Press. 1995.

Elion, L.K. *Chuck Baird, 35 Plates*. California: DawnSignPress. 1993.

Hairston, Ernest & Smith, Linwood. *Black and Deaf in America: Are We That Different?*. Maryland: T.J. Publishers, Inc. 1983.

Hepner, Cheryl. *Seeds of Disquiet*. Washington, DC: Gallaudet University Press. 1987.

Gannon, Jack. *Deaf Heritage*. Maryland: National Association of the Deaf. 1981.

Gannon, Jack. *The Week the World Heard Gallaudet*. Washington, DC: Gallaudet University Press. 1989.

Groce, Nora. *Everyone Here Spoke Sign Language: Hereditary Deafness on Martha's Vineyard*. Massachusetts: Harvard University Press. 1985.

Hay, John A. & Lee, Raymond. *A Pictorial History of the Evolution of the British Manual Alphabet*. British Deaf Historical Society. 1994.

Holcomb, Majoriebell & Wood, Sharon. *Deaf Women: A Parade Through the Decades*. California: DawnSignPress. 1989.

International Conference on Deaf History, British Deaf Heritage, Peter Jackson. Maryland: Sign Media Inc. 1992. Videotape.

Jackson, Peter. *Britain's Deaf Heritage*. Scotland: Pentland Press. 1990.

Johnson, Robert C., Snider, Bruce & Erting, Carol. *Readings in the Language, Culture, History, and Arts of Deaf People: Selected Papers from the Deaf Way Conference*. Washington, DC: Gallaudet University Press. 1995.

Lang, Harry, and Bonnie Meath-Lang, *Deaf Persons in the Arts and Science: a Biographical Dictionary*. Westport, Connecticut: Greenwood Press. 1995.

Lane, Harlan, *When the Mind Hears: A History of the Deaf*. New York: Random House. 1984. *A History of the Deaf: When the Mind Hears*. Maryland: Sign Media Inc. 1993. Videotape.

Lane, Harlan, Hoffmeister, Robert, & Bahan, Ben. *A Journey into the DEAF–WORLD*. California: DawnSignPress. 1996.

Lucas, Ceil. *Sociolinguistics in Deaf Communities*, Vol. 2. Washington, DC: Gallaudet University Press. 1996.

Lucas, Ceil. *The Sociolinguistics of the Deaf Community*. New York: Academic Press. 1989.

National Federation of the Blind, 1800 Johnson St., Suite 300, Baltimore, MD 21230-4998.

Padden, Carol & Humphries, Tom. *Deaf in America–Voices from a Culture*. Massachusetts: Harvard University Press. 1988.

Panara, Robert & Panara, John. *Great Deaf Americans*. Maryland: T.J. Publishers, Inc. 1983.

Preston Paul, Mother Father Deaf: Living between Sound and Silence. Massachusetts: Harvard University Press. 1994.

Schein, Jerome. *A Rose for Tomorrow: A Biography of Frederick C. Schreiber*. Maryland: National Association of the Deaf. 1981.

Smith, Linwood. *Silence, Love, and Kids I Know: Poems*. Washington, DC: International Books. 1977.

Valli, Clayton & Lucas, Ceil. *Linguistics of American Sign Language: An Introduction*. Gallaudet University Press, Washington, D.C. 1990. Text and videotape.

Van Cleve, John & Crouch, Barry. *A Place of Their Own: Creating the Deaf Community in America*. Washington, DC: Gallaudet University Press. 1989.

Van Cleve, John. Ed., Encyclopedia on Deafness. New York: McGraw-Hill Co. Inc. 1987.

Wilcox, Sherman. *American Deaf Culture: An Anthology*. Maryland: Linstok Press. 1989.

Winefield, Richard. *Never the Twain Shall Meet: The Communications Debate*. Washington, DC: Gallaudet University Press. 1987.

FINGERSPELLING, GESTURES, SIGN LANGUAGES

A special category of "Deaf Culture" includes materials that relate to gestures, signs, and sign languages.

A Pictorial History of the Evolution of the British Manual Alphabet, Hay, John A. & Lee, Raymond, *British Deaf Historical Society*. 1994.

The ABC Stories Sign Media Inc., 4020 Blackburn Lane, Burtonsville, MD 20866, 1-800-475-4756. Videotape.

The ASL Handshape Game Cards, DawnSignPress, 6130 Nancy Ridge Road, San Diego, CA. 1-800-549-5350.

Axtell, Roger E. *Gestures: The DO's and TABOOs of Body Language Around the World*. New York: John Wiley & Sons, Inc. 1991.

Baker, Charlotte & Cokely, Dennis. *American Sign Language: A Teacher's Resource Text on Grammar and Culture*. Maryland: T.J. Publishers, Inc. 1980.

Carmel, Simon. *International Hand Alphabet Charts*. Maryland: Studio Printing, Inc. 20851. 1982.

Eastman, Gilbert. *From Mime to Sign*. Maryland: T.J. Publishers. 1989.

Klima Edward & Bellugi, Ursula. *The Signs of Language*. New York: Harvard University Press. 1979.

Lentz, Ella Mae. *The Treasure*. In Motion Press. 1995.

Liddell, Scott. *American Sign Language Syntax*. New York: Mouton Publishers. 1980.

Madsen, Willard. *Conversational Sign Language II*. Washington, DC: Gallaudet University Press. 1972.

Miles, Dorothy. *British Sign Language–A Beginner's Guide*. London: BBC Books. 1988.

Moody, Bill. *La Langue Des Signe: Dictionnaire Bilingue Elementaire, Tome 1*. France: International Visual Theatre. 1986.

Moody, Bill. *La Langue Des Signe: Dictionnaire Bilingue Elementaire, Tome 2*. France: International Visual Theatre. 1986.

Poetry in Motion. Sign Media Inc., 4020 Blackburn Lane, Burtonsville, MD. 20866. Videotape.

Supalla, Samuel. *The Book of Name Signs*. California: DawnSignPress. 1992.

Valli, Clayton, *ASL Poetry, Selected Works by Clayton Valli*. California: DawnSignPress. 1995. Text and videotape.

HUMOR

These books involve language and culture—and they are funny, too.

Holcomb, Ray, Holcomb, Samuel & Holcomb, Thomas. *Deaf Culture, Our Way: Anecdotes from the Deaf Community*. California: DawnSignPress. 1995.

Holcomb, Ray, Rolfe, Ray & Bahan, Ben J. *Silence is Golden, Sometimes*. California: DawnSignPress. 1985.

Holcomb, Ray. *Hazards of Deafness*. California: Joyce Media, Inc. 1977.

Glickman, Ken. *Deafinitions for Signlets*. Maryland: DiKen Products. 1987.

Glickman, Ken. *More Deafinitions*. Maryland: DiKen Products. 1989.

DEAF ORGANIZATIONS

These agencies of specialized advocacy and activity are run primarily by and for Deaf people.

United States of America Deaf Sports Federation, P.O. Box 22011, Santa Fe, NM 87502.

Association of Late-Deafened Adults, 8038 Macintosh Lane, Suite 2, Rockford, IL 61107.

Children of Deaf Adult(s), CODA, 41041 Trimboli Way #1788, Fremont, CA 94538.

Deaf Artists of America, 302 N. Goodman St. Suite 205, Rochester, NY 14607.

Deaf Women United, Inc., P.O. Box 91765, Washington, DC 20090.

National Association of the Deaf, Jr. National Association of the Deaf, Youth Leadership Camp, 8630 Fenton Street, Suite 820, Silver Spring, MD 20910.

National Black Deaf Advocates, P.O. Box 564, Secane, PA 19018.

National Theatre of the Deaf, 139 North Main Street, West Hartford, CT 06107.

Rainbow Alliance of the Deaf, 5014 LaHoma, Dallas, TX 75235.

Self-Help for Hard-of-Hearing People, 7910 Woodmont Ave. Suite 1200, Bethesda, MD 20814.

Telecommunications for the Deaf Incorporated, P.O. Box 8009, Silver Spring, MD 20907.

World Recreation Association of the Deaf, P.O. Box 3211, Quartz Hill, CA 93586.

CAPTIONING SERVICES

These agencies provide and assist with provision of captioning for TV, film, and videotape.

Caption It!, 400 Andrews St. Suite 510, Rochester, NY 14604.

Florida Captioning Services, 8429 N. 70th East Avenue, Owasso, OK 74055.

National Captioning Institute, 3725 Concorde Pkwy, Suite 100, Chantilly, VA 20151.

The Caption Center, 125 Western Ave, Boston, MA 02134.

VITAC, 8300 East Maplewood Avenue, Suite 310, Greenwood Village, CO 80111.

NEWSPAPERS & MAGAZINES

Just a few of the publications that we enjoy.

Deaf Life, MSM Productions, LTD, 1095 Meigs Street, Rochester, NY 14620.

Silent News, 133 Gaither Dr. Suite E, Mount Laurel, NJ 08054-1710.

Deaf Nation, P.O. Box 2444, Birmingham, MI 48012.

ENGLISH REFERENCES

English as a second language users will find these materials especially helpful.

Berstein, Theodore M. *The Careful Writer: A Modern Guide to English* Usage. New York: Macmillan. 1965.

Corbeil, Jean-Claude. *Visual Dictionary*. Canada: Facts on Files. 1986.

Stenton, Adrian (ed.) *Longman Dictionary of American English: A Dictionary for Learners of American English*. White Plains, NY: Longman. 1983.

Hall, Eugene J. *Dictionary of Prepositions: For Students of English*. New York: Minerva Books. 1982.

Makkai Adam, Boatner, Maxine, & Gates, John, *Handbook of Commonly Used Idioms*. New York: Barron's Educational Services Inc. 1984.

Pheby, John (ed.) *Pictorial English Dictionary*. Hong Kong: Oxford University Press. 1981.

Sinclair, John (ed.) *English Language Dictionary*. Reprint. Great Britain: Collins, Sons & Co. 1990.

STORYTELLERS & HUMORISTS

Just a few of the excellent Deaf performers we know.

Evon Black, 9306 Edmonston Road, Greenbelt, MD 20815.

Robert Daniels, P.O. Box 4627, Alexander, VA 22303.

Ken Glickman, "Prof. Glick," DEAFinitely Yours Studio, 814 Thayer Ave. Suite 305, Silver Spring, MD 20910-4500.

Charles "C.J." Jones, 5810 Las Virgenes Rd., Calbasa, CA 91302.

NOTES

NOTES

NOTES

NOTES

NOTES

NOTES